GROWING UP
IN THE WEST END OF
NEW ROCHELLE,
NEW YORK IN THE 50's-60's

CONTENTS

INTRODUCTION

Why did I want to write this book? I thought about why?
What made me say to myself "I want to write about the Old
neighborhood "West New Rochelle"? The answer is very simple.
I felt a compassionate fever of expressing the social atmosphere
of a simple neighboring life. Directed towards love, passion, good
friendships, looking out for your neighbors, playing in the streets
and just good ole Ma-Pa family life with Ma-Pa business stores.

The "West End" of New Rochelle, NY when I was growing up was
considered diverse. Of course the majority of the neighborhood was
Italian immigrants with the children becoming Italian-Americans.
The neighborhood also was blessed with very nice Irish, Jewish and
African-American families. *Yes we all got along.* I cannot remember any
wrong doing or disrespect among neighbors or another ethnic group.
It just didn't happen. Why? I'm not sure. The times like I said were
simple, fun, enjoyable with good ole family neighbors and families!

The book will explain in my terms "The West" when I was growing
up. All the people, friends and families that made it such a memorable
and lasting creation and foundation of childhood, youth, as an
adolescent right up to my High School years. The book will explain
the neighborhood where we all played, shopped, bought our baseballs,
lemon ice, candy, newspapers, bologna sandwiches, pizza or just hung
out. Our neighborhood schools, church, restaurants, grocery stores etc.

Hopefully my memories, reflection and experiences of "The West" will bring you joy and many great memories like I have endured!

Good Reading to You as I Return You To:
~ "Growing Up in the West End of New Rochelle in the 50's-60's" ~
The way I Remember it!....~ My Memoirs ~.... *Dennis M. Nardone*

Dedicated To:

My Dad—Tony "Sonny Boy"
My Mom—Esther "Est"
My Brother—Anthony Jr. "Butch"
My Sister—Diane "Di"
To all my Family, Friends and Neighbors
of the "West End of New Rochelle, N.Y"
who dedicated their lives to hard work
to support there families....
To all those who came to America
to find a better life....
To all who found it "up The West"

*All proceeds or any monetary value gained
from selling this book after all expenses paid
will be donated to Saint Joseph Church
located on Washington Ave in the
"West End" of New Rochelle, N.Y.
Dennis M. Nardone
Author*

Those who contributed to assist in writing this book by offering
Information, Pictures or just General Knowledge of
"The West End" of New Rochelle, NY

Eileen Mason—Editing
Ron Tocci
Peter Parente
Margaret Rainone-Bauer
Fran Datillo
Frank Miceli
Tony Monteleone
Danny Costa
Tom Savoca
Anthony Galletta
John McGuire
World Wide Web Internet

Who do Recognize?

The Original "West End Original's"
Little Marco in the Middle (White Shirt)

Marco Petrozzi & Marco Lacerenza
(AKA Little Marco & Big Marco)
"West End Originals"
(Standing In Feeney Park)

My Two Childhood Friends—Pix taken 2006
Mauro Viccaro—Dennis—Danny Costa

CHAPTER (1)

"Up the West" or as some call it "West New Rochelle"

The boundary lines of "West New Rochelle" are considered by many people as divided into two separate sections which are divided by Webster Ave.

The first section of "West New Rochelle" starts with the NORTH boundary line—Webster Ave. Webster Ave runs from Jones Street to Sickles Ave. The corner stone is at the Old Carvel stand which stood for many years with the huge ice cream cone on the roof. It is now just a plain old regular square carvel store mixed in with a row of other stores.

The West boundary line is Sickles Ave. Sickles Ave runs from Webster Ave to Madeline Ave to Feeney Park.

The SOUTH boundary line is the Village of Pelham border. The last streets of the "West" would be Eight & Ninth Streets.

Now the EAST boundary line would be the New Haven Railroad Tracks. Street wise it would be Fifth, Fourth, Third and Second Street connecting into Lafayette Ave which runs parallel with the railroad tracks. At Second Street and Jones Street, starting at Rocco Bellantoni's Grocery Store (The store is actually on Second St.) which would be the EAST border connection from Second St. back to the start at Webster Ave.

The second connection that is in question are the streets north of Webster Ave up to the Casa Calabria Italian Club. Many people feel and still considered that portion "West New Rochelle." Some would argue that it is not part of "West New Rochelle." I really do not know how important it is to be or not to be part of the "West." All those streets like Washington Ave, Union Ave are all part of the "West" to me!

The section in doubt according to my father is considered part of "West New Rochelle."…..So right or wrong, or it is or isn't, as a kid growing up, if my father said it was part of the "West" then that was good enough for me!

Again the EAST boundary line is the railroad tracks or the new England Thruway (I-95) or Grove Ave that runs parallel with the Thruway. The streets connected to grove Ave are Walnut, Warren etc.

The NORTH boundary border line is Warren St. but no further then the Casa Calabria Italian Social Club which is located on the corner of Warren St. and Union Ave.

Washington Ave to Webster Ave would be the WEST boundary border line.

The SOUTH border line is Webster Ave from Jones St. & Grove Ave to Washington Ave.

So whatever you feel, if the 2nd section is considered "West New Rochelle." Then so be it. In your eyes it's considered part of "West New Rochelle. Whatever anyone thoughts were in their interpretation of the boundary lines for "West New Rochelle," it sure made for many Sunday morning corner discussions from Union Ave & Fifth Street to the corner of the Casa Calabria Social Club. Many Sunday mornings you could hear the Italian language going a mile a minute with a circle of men all talking at the same time. Cigarettes, pipes, cigars with bellowing smoke while the hands and arms flaring in the air!

My mother always said all those men talked the same stories every week trying to convince the other guy his story.

Getting back to the boundary lines. *Really,* is their any importance to what is "West" New Rochelle or not? Some say yes, some say no.

One thing is for sure. Their must be some sort of importance because through the years the political powers often found ways to re-align the district lines to help favor the vote of what party happened to be in power. The adjustment of the district lines proved the voice of the neighborhood to be a strong advocate to the potential winner.

Chapter (2)

"The Homes, the Landscape and the Neighborhood"

For the most part "West New Rochelle" is relatively old homes, usually two, three family homes. Built somewhere at the turn of the century. Most of the houses are built close to each other. Some separated by a small alley walkway. Some with no front lawn. The homes built right up to the sidewalk. Oh yes, the old sidewalks. Big 4'x3' gray slate plates. Great for playing hop scotch. Most homes had a porch in front. Most of the homes built with wood frames. Some were stucco, some were just plain old cement. The two, three story apartment buildings were decorated with a façade that no longer are used in the architecture when building homes these days. Beautiful designed frames that the architect of that day who took pride in designing the building.

Of course the homes with a nice lawn were all groomed like a fine upscale golf course. Each home no matter how old always took pride in the landscape. The grass always green, cut to a crop, green bushes trimmed to a style of delight to all the neighbors. Many of the homes were decorated with an iron clad fence around the yard or home.

The "West New Rochelle" neighborhood how I remember it in the late 1950's and through the 1960's is something I wish that a lot of people could have experienced while growing up. I hope wherever you may have grown up you may have fond memories of families, friends, neighbors, schools, holidays, huge snow storms, taking out that baseball glove (that you received as a Christmas present) in the early days of spring and hitting that ball soon as the afternoon school bell rang. Riding your brand new schwinn bicycle or the new 3 speed. In the summer the sprinklers in the park and open fire hydrants in the streets were gushing out like your own Niagara Falls!

In the fall, playing in the pile of leaves. Shaking chestnuts from the trees at the Beechwood Cemetery and then tying them to a string and see who can break the other guys chestnut first by swinging at it and hitting it with your chestnut until the other guys chestnut would break. We would have some great battle of the chestnuts! We would soak our chestnuts in some sort of oil to harden them and then name your chestnut like Hercules or Sampson. *Man good ole days....*

Of course there were the cold crisp days of playing tackle football with no helmets or padding. Just good ole hitting and knocking your friend on his butt. Myself and Danny Costa would jump over the fence onto his dad's lawn when his mom was cleaning the house downstairs and have some real banged up one on one games for hours.

The winters were great. Real snow storms. Jump out of bed as soon as WVOX Radio would mention "All New Rochelle School's Closed." get out there and grab a shovel and knock on doors or ask someone if they need help shoveling their car out to make a buck. Then there were the neighborhood snow ball fights! Danny and I would build our snow fort on the hill of (again) his dads lawn and wait for cars to come up and down the hill of Fifth St. & Lafayette Ave and throw snow balls at the cars.

No one really locked doors back then. If you did the key was under the door mat. When you knocked on your neighbor's door they would yell "Who is it"?—"Come on in"—with out hesitation to look or to see who it was!....Good times, yes, rough times, yes but simple, exciting and full of love!

In the warm months, all through the neighborhood everyone sat outside. No, not in the backyards but in front of the house. That was so the parents could keep a good eye on their kids playing in the streets. Some had their porch, who had there bench or chairs.

There where stoops and steps. If you were under the age of 12 you stood in front of the house. You played catch, maybe a little wiffle-ball.

The girls marked the sidewalks and played hopscotch. In the streets you could find a good game of kickball with the telephone pole as first base. The sewer cover man hole in the middle of the street as second base. The "No Parking" Sign (alternate street parking for the street sweeper) was third base. Then of course you would draw a beautiful home plate with bright white chalk.

There were the kids on the bicycles, roller skates playing games like hide and go-seek, Nut-it etc.

Saturday morning was the big card games among us kids. Man we would get four or five guys and play touches with our baseball cards. You can play 1-touch or up to 10 touches. You would fling the card and touch the other kids card. We also played the game where you would stand the card up against the wall and try to knock it down. Of course only the "stinky non-good baseball player cards were used." NO Yankees (Mickey Mantle card, man that was the best!!)... Although if you got triples of some Yankee cards that was OK to play with. But NO Mantle, Berra, Maris, Richardson, Kubek, Lopez, Howard, or first string Yankee players or other All-Star team cards like Mays, the Duke, Killabrew, Kaline, Boyer, McCovey, Koufax etc. etc.

Union Ave looking towards 8th Street

"Parade"
Union Ave
Near
Charles St.

Union Ave looking on 2nd St.
Old Caruso Supermarket on
right "Pershing Sq." Building
in distance.

Street Pix

My Two Childhood Friends - Pix taken 2006
Mauro Viccaro - Dennis - Danny Costa

Actor Vincent Pastore from the "West"

Alexander "Sonny Mecca" Rotina

Obituary

Rotina, Alexander "Sonny Mecca"

Alexander "Sonny Mecca" Rotina passed away on August 19, 2011. He was born on August 15, 1920 to Louis and Mary Mecca Rotina. Survived by sister Angelina Sarachelli, nephew Paul (Maria) Sarachelli, niece Jean (Tommy) Diluro, great nephews Paul Sarachelli, III and Michael Diluro, great niece Stephania Sarachelli. Predeceased by his brother-in-law Paul Sarachelli.

Born and raised in West New Rochelle, Sonny, 91, loved his neighborhood, especially St. Joseph's Church and the Feeney Park Boys Club, where he was a volunteer for many years. His favorite hobbies were roller skating, playing the harmonica and watching Lawrence Welk. He loved to recall the old days at the Feeney Park Boys Club where Gus Mascaro and Hank DeClemente befriended him. He worked at the Bonnie Briar Country Club as a caddy where he retired in 1985. He enjoyed carrying the flag at the St. Anthony's feast every year at St. Joseph's Church. He loved holidays and family get togethers and especially loved his sister Angelina who loyally took care of him for many years. His smile and loving good nature was a gift to his family and friends for 91 years especially to all of his nieces and nephews; whom he was very proud of and was a very special part of their lives. Last year, a large gathering of family and friends joyfully celebrated his 90th birthday. His family and friends will dearly miss him but he will remain in their hearts forever. May he rest in peace in a high place in heaven which he truly deserves.

Me-Mauro-Danny/Pastore/Sonny

Chapter (3)

"Where I Was Born"

July 17th 1951, I was born in New Rochelle Hospital somewhere around 3am to Anthony Nardone & Esther Iscaro Nardone. I was the third child born in the family. Ahead of me was my older brother Anthony Jr. eight years older. My sister Diane is the middle child. We are all four years apart. My mother named me Dennis and always said enough with the Anthony's, Michael's, Joseph's and the Italian names in the family. Not that she was against the Italian tradition but she just thought how many of the same Italian names in the family are you going to have. So with that she went Irish and Dennis it was. As a kid growing up I wanted the name "Roy" after my childhood hero TV cowboy star Roy Rogers. I would have even settled for "Roger." I thought maybe I could adapt a nickname by being called "Roy" or "Roger" but my mother wasn't going for it. I even tried to be called "Mickey" for my other hero "Mickey Mantle" but nooo as I said mom was not going for it. She wasn't keen on nicknames although my brother was called "Butch" only because of all the "Anthony's" in the family and my father was called "Sonny Boy." My sister kinda had a nickname. Long before "Lady Di from England my sister was always called "Di."

We were all born on the corner of Union Ave & 7th Street, 316 Union Ave to be exact. Known as the Immediato flat. If I remember it had three stories. We lived on the second floor. It is an old red brick building with the building front built right up to the front sidewalk. The left side was

Grandma Immediato who had a grocery store. Grandma Immediato lived in the back of the grocery store. A sheet would separate the apartment from the store. Grandma Immediato was into her late 70's when I was 5 or 6 years old. She would always drop the coins and they would roll under the counter. She couldn't bend to pick them up so she would just leave them there.

So later in the day I would sneak in and look under the counter and reach under and come up with all kinds of pennies, nickels, dimes, quarters and at times get real lucky and find a silver dollar. I would then run over to Cannata's on the corner of Union Ave & 6th Street. "Rossi" grandmother had a dusty old little candy store. I couldn't go far so I would buy my candy there.

If I had change left over and my mom found it, she would say with that stern look "You have been reaching under the counter again"—"I told you not to do that"—and of course like any good little boy I would say in my little cute face "I'm sorry mom I won't do it again." Then as she left the room I would take my candy out from the hiding place (a sock) and have a feast!

Grandma Immediato's grocery store eventually closed up and became another apartment when she passed on but we had moved out by then.

On the first floor Grandma Immediato's family lived on the other side of the hall from the grocery store. Their was Camille (that was my age and I went to school with), Carmine and Eugene.

When you walked into the building from the sidewalk. I remember a huge hallway with wide stairs and with a banister that the mahogany wood was so thick, shiny and slippery. You could jump and sit on it from the upper floors and with no hands slide three floors down. When you came to the bottom 1st floor the railing would end up in a swivel kind of swerve and it looked like something from the movie "Gone with the Wind."

But while sliding down you had to be real careful and you had to be ready to jump off when you got to the bottom because if you didn't you slid right into the crown of the banister and man did that hurt!

The basement or cellar as we called it was as creepy and scary as anything that I can remember. Right out of some scary movie. Everything was filled with cobwebs. Old wood with little built storage areas. The best was the shower! Yes the tenants would go to the cellar to shower. This nasty old stall with a long string or rope hanging down. Of course I took a bath in the kitchen sink. Then all of a sudden we had tubs! Those big old fancy tubs up on it's legs. No showers in the apartments. We are talking about somewhere around 1956.

We had a big yard. But it was filled with piles of wood all over the place. For what, I don't know. But their would be stacks of 2x4's and stacks of plywood. The wood would be warped and ruined by the rain and weather. But I do remember the pear tree we had. It would grow some very tasty pears. There also was a fig tree that in the winter it had to be wrapped like a mummy to keep it fresh for the next season. My father would wrap that fig tree maybe two feet thick full of I guess blankets and tarp paper and whatever else to keep the bad weather element from destroying the fig tree. It would kind of start to bend like a banana. But come the next season that tree would have good tasting delicious juicy figs.

There also was a garage. We never went in the garage. I don't remember who used it but again it was filled with piles of wood!

On the third floor lived my Godfather Nick Circelli (who baptized me), Rose and their son Salvatore, known as Sal.

One day Sal took me in the yard to teach me how to throw darts. I was about 4 or 5 years old and Sal was in his teens. Sal threw the darts at the board that he set up on the garage. He then said here hold these darts let me get the other darts that he threw. Well I didn't wait as I threw a dart and it landed and stuck right into his neck...Sal yelled so loud that I ran away.....But he was Ok after that.....*No more darts!*

Godfather Nick never drove a car, never had a driver's license that I always thought was peculiar. In those day's very few ladies or wives drove cars so the man of the house always drove a car. But Nick said he never wanted a car. He always worked in factories of some sort as I remember and always close to the area in walking distance.

Nick loved music and fishing. He would take me fishing to Glen Island and show me how to fish with three hooks. He taught me how to cast a line. It took me awhile to learn how to cast because I was holding onto the line with my finger too long and "snap" would go the hook and sinker flying to the middle of the water. In time I was able to tie a hook, sinker and hook a worm and then "wham" cast like a pro. He would teach me and tell me about the tides and when fish would come in and out and the best time to catch them. We would always fish for flounder, I have to say, he knew the sport well. He was a great fisherman. He could catch three fish at a time. Nick would see the line pull and the rod bend and say OK there's one now lets wait for the second and third to bite the other hooks. When that fishing rod bent over he would grab the rod and reel in the fish and yes there they were. Three big juicy flounders flapping like crazy. Now me on the other hand I was lucky to get a nibble and if I got lucky I would catch one or two small fish then I would have to throw them back.

I remember one time I reeled in "Sea Robin" fish. That fish was so ugly that it scared the heck out of me! I didn't know what it was and I ended up dropping the fishing rod on the ground and it almost went in the water! Godfather Nick lashed at me and had a few choice words that weren't so pleasant sounding as he picked up the rod. It was the first time he got mad at me. But I couldn't blame him he took care of his equipment and I just dropped it on the ground. But, man was I scared of that fish, it was horrible looking!.... Anyway, for now on I was very careful and respectful of Godfather Nick's fishing equipment.

When we got home from fishing Nick would always tell my mom and dad how I caught the biggest fish. Of course they would play it off and make a fuss and like a little fool I would believe that my mom and dad thought I caught all those big fish. But I loved to go fishing with Godfather Nick. Rosy (Nick's wife) would pack us lunch. Two bologna sandwiches on white bread. Nick would have a container of coffee and I would drink milk. We always went to the same spot and sat on the same rocks. Now of course there are no more rocks. A nice pier with a railing was built all around Glen Island. To this day when I go to Glen Island I look to the spot and reminisce about those childhood days with my Godfather.... Thank You Nick!

Nick had a huge selection and collection of Rod & Reels, fishing tackle and all kind of equipment. He had everything stacked and hanging so neatly in the cellar behind the wooded gate that looked like some old horse barn with chicken wire around it.

He had short, long, thin, thick fishing rods for all kind of different fishing. Some for salt water, some for fresh water etc. He was a true fisherman.

He then taught me how to clean the fish by cutting off the head and tail and scrapping the scales and washing them so they can be cooked. My mother was great at cooking the fish. But she hated cleaning them. She would always say. "You caught them now you clean them if you want to eat the fish." So she would bread them in egg and bread crumbs, maybe a little wine or cooking oil. She then baked them in the oven and at times fry them on the stove in a pan. Whatever which way, man did they taste good! We had to be careful of the bones. Although my mother was good at cutting and filleting the fish. You always had to be very careful of a bone here and there. But mmmm did they taste delicious.

Godfather Nick was always very good to me. He loved telling me stories about his family and the neighborhood that I always felt were very interesting. Nick never missed my birthday. Nick and his wife Rosey would always give me my traditional big chocolate (hollow) bunny for Easter and they would never ever miss Christmas.

Godfather Nick loved music. I think that was the start of my love for music. My mom and dad were not big music lovers except for the variety TV Shows like Dean Martin, Perry Como, Andy Williams and of course they loved watching Ed Sullivan on Sunday Nights. But as for playing the radio or records it just didn't happen with mom and dad. Of course my brother Anthony and my sister Diane played the radio and records all day long which was also a big influence on me for the love of music and also an education of different singers and music.

But Nick would sit me in the living room all through my child and teen years and play records for me. He taught me about "Stereo" and how to separate the speakers for the "surround sound" as it was first introduced. He would play a record and say "OK where are the speakers?"—I would look around and say "I don't know?"—Nick then would show me they were behind the couch or chair. He would also teach me the value of records and how to handle and hold them. He would show me how to clean and watch for scratches. He didn't buy 45's records, only LP's. 45's records he would say are for kids. 45's records of course were the small version record with usually a "A" side one song and a "B" side one song. They had the big hole in the middle about an inch in diameter so music lovers like my sister could stack the 45's records maybe 10-15 in a pile on the Victrola. Did I say "Victrola", yes the record player that was built like a box.

When you open the lid you would see a round disc with a fat tube going down the middle and a swinging arm that would rest on the stack of records. Then there was the other arm with the diamond needle that would at the time be a big electronic break through! The arm would swing onto the record by itself and the needle would set itself on the record and music or a voice would play and be heard. There was a little switch in the back so you can change the RPM's from 45 to 44 to 78 depending on the record size. That system of stacking records and using a Victrola was great for those teenager basement party's. You didn't have to run and put a record on every time the song ended especially when things were getting close! You would have enough music for at least 45 minutes. The only problem back then, songs were maybe two and half to three minutes long. LP's stood for Long Playing record. A collection of songs in what they call an album of music. The hole in the middle of the LP was maybe a quarter of in inch in diameter so of course to get more songs on the record. The number 45 and 78 stood for RPM. Rotates Per Minute. Records were made of vinyl material and Nick would show me how to maintain the records because if you weren't careful you could find warped or wobbly records. This could result from heat if stored to close to a radiator or get ruined by having them near windows etc. Nick would also like to show me his old collection of 78's. The big thick vinyl record. His collection was Big Band, Swing, Jimmy Durante. He loved Italian singers. His collection of music and records went far back to the thirties. He loved it all!

Godfather Nick was a funny guy!—A dry sense of humor type. He would say to his wife Rose "Your nuttier then a fruit cake" and I would laugh like crazy. Rosey would say to me "Don't laugh at his stupid remarks that makes you nuttier then me!"—*All in Fun!*

Godfather Nick's wife was Rose Circelli or as we called her "Rosey." Rosey was a lady that everyone loved. Bubbly, funny and the wife and mother that would do everything around the house for her husband and son. She was a replica of "Ethel Mort" (Vivian Vance the actress from the "I Love Lucy" TV show. (My mother was "Lucy" with her red hair, blue eyes and funny Lucille Ball face antics.)

Rosey was a cleanliness fanatic. Everything spic and span. Eat off the floors as they say. She had the kind of personality where she would do those innocent little dumb things or say those innocent little things that you just shook your head to but made you laugh for ever. Of course Nick would say "Nutter then a fruit cake." They were just a great pair together.

Nothing like Sunday Morning and Mom frying the Meatballs and getting ready for our Sunday Macaroni afternoon Dinner

I ❤️
MEATBALLS

GRAVY!
Not Sauce...

MEATBALLS & SOME OF MY FAVORITE DISHES

Ravioli

Lasagna

Meatballs

Rosey would cook meatballs that had a tantalizing aroma that just drove you crazy. As a child I would sneak up to the third floor and Rosey would cut the meatball into 4 pieces. I would love to eat it with no gravy on it. Then I would sneak back down to the apartment. I thought as a little kid I was getting over. But mom and Rosey had it all planned. It took awhile but I found out years later.

Rosey also loved making "Cold Cut Meat" sandwiches for everyone. Cold cut meat is sliced lunch meat. The kind of deli meat that is sliced on a meat slicer. She loved Mortadella, Proscuitto, Ham, Olive Loaf and Provolone Cheese. She would buy the fresh kaiser rolls from Millie's on Union Ave and invite everyone over for sandwiches. When I reached my teens and I was working the "Cold Cut" counter at Daylight Meateria on Main St., New Rochelle across from the RCA Proctor Movie Theater (Where my Mother & Brother-In-Law Tony worked) Rosey would come in on Saturday and have me slice her cold cuts. And yes I did throw on a few more slices over the half a pond line.

Sal&Ro

Dad&Me/Sis&Me

CHAPTER (4)

"Dad—Mom—Brother—Sister"

My Father Anthony Nardone Sr.

Dad's Navy Pix

Dad came over from Italy with my Uncle Sam, Uncle Frank (Cheech), Uncle Armand and Aunt Rita. They came from the Naples section of Italy before World War II. My father was about 15-16 years old when he came to America. He never had any formal education in the states as the family migrated to the "West" New Rochelle. Like many Italian men my father took up landscaping and cement work but settled for the landscaping. He even had his own business for awhile. But being more of a worker it didn't work out because my father was too kind to charge too much money and really didn't keep up with the paper work either.

My father had a very unique personality. Never a strong bearing voice, he would rather help and do things for people then get paid. Anything anyone would want he would go out of his way to get it for them. I'm not talking going out and purchase products. I'm talking physical work, or if he was able to get flowers, shrubbery he would find a way to get it for you.

My father was a heck of a cook or I should say chef. He loved to cook. All I remember that he loved cooking all types of beans each and every way he can. Of course pasta was #1. My mother would go crazy because no matter what mom cooked for dinner he had to have some sort of macaroni on the side. Be it linguini, spaghetti, ziti, pastina etc. He would make it with butter, maybe tomato sauce or just whip up some sort of topping. My sister didn't eat much of the pasta unless it was macaroni night and on Sunday for a specialty like ravioli, manicotti, stuffed shells etc. My favorite even to this day is fusilli. My sister loves fusilli as well. Wednesday night was always spaghetti night. Anyway, my brother and I would always say yes to the pasta on the side. I know what your thinking, yes I LOVE MACARONI. I can eat it everyday!

Saturday night became Chinese Dinner night. They didn't have Chinese take out restaurants then like they do now. So my father would drive to Larchmont or Pelham and pick up the order. All we ate was chicken chow-mein. It wasn't until I was maybe 16 before I found out their were other Chinese dishes. But every Saturday it was chicken chow-mein with of course white rice. On Friday we would have pizza pie from Viccaro's Pizza Parlor located on Union Ave. between Fifth St & Sixth St. I would go pick it up. But when you went to Viccaro's for a take out order you had to pick up your order from the bar section and man you would walk in and to the left was the bar counter with about 10 stools and to the right were a few tables where the men would drink and play cards. It looked like a scene from the TV show "Gunsmoke"—They even had swinging cowboy style doors going into the kitchen area. The place was bellowing with cigarettes, cigars and clouds of smoke! It was a heck of a salon but the restaurant and food was the best. (More about Viccaro's later on in the book.)

My father loved to go Mushroom picking. He had a knack for knowing which mushroom's to pick because you had to be careful and know which mushroom's were safe to eat or you can be poisoned or make you very sick. Dad would go out in the fall season and come back with bags full of these big white mushroom's. My father and my Godmother Francis Guida Iscaro who lived down stairs from us on 9 Fifth St. (by now the family had moved from Seventh St. & Union Ave. to 9 Fifth St.) would spend all night cleaning them and jarring them in water in these sealed bottles that had a rubber and metal clip to keep them air tight. They would examine every mushroom checking every part and bit of it for discoloration and bugs. But I got to tell you, when they were cleaned, cut & fried up or cooked they were absolutely the best tasting mushrooms you would ever eat anywhere!

My father served in the Navy during World War II. He was assigned as a Cook on a ship (Tanker) stationed in the Pacific. He gained the rank of 2nd Class Petty Officer. My father was so proud of the fact that he served in the United States Navy and often spoke about it for many years. He loved to reminisce while watching the old black & white war moves especially if it was about WWII. My mother would always tease him by saying "You were only a Cook." and my father would reply by saying "Yes, but a 2nd Class Petty Officer." So my mother would then tease him more by saying "they only gave you that rank because you cooked for the Captain of the ship during off hours." It became a long standing joke for many years whenever family or new friends were visiting.

I would always ask my father what was the name of the ship that he served on. Because of his heavy Italian accent he would never say the name correct. I never found out the name until a gentleman came to my fathers wake at Cancro's Funeral Parlor to pay his respects. The gentleman introduced himself and said "I saw your father's name in the newspaper. I always wondered whatever happened to your father." "I knew he lived in Westchester County and I'm sorry that I never got to talk with him."—"I felt bad and had to come to the funeral parlor." The gentleman served in the Navy with my father. He told me if I was half the man my father was you have to be a great guy. He said my father was loved by everyone and that he was good to everyone. He would feed you at anytime and do whatever he could for anyone. "Just a great guy"—"lots of fun"....I asked him what do you mean by fun as I was trying to see what my father might have been like when he was in his 20's and in the Navy. The gentleman said—"You know a young guy in the Navy"—He said did you ever play sports and hang with guys and I'm sure you were young at one time! So I kinda got the jest of what he was saying.

I told the gentleman that my father was never able to tell me the name of the ship because of his heavy Italian accent and if he can tell me the name. He told me the name of the ship was the U.S. CACAPON AO-52—So I asked him what does that mean and he said it was a tanker that was stationed in the Pacific Ocean and that it's purpose was to fuel the battleships out on the ocean. The tanker would sail in between the fleet but it was a dangerous boat because the enemy would try to blow it up so not to fuel the Battleships and that would cause a major problem at sea. He then asked me if my father ever received his war medals that were awarded to the ship? I said I never seen any medals and I'm sure he would have shown us if he did.

A few weeks after the funeral I wrote the pentagon in Washington D.C. and told the Navy about my father and about six months later six medals came in the mail for me. I just wish he could have seen them. He would have probably worn those medals every day that's how proud he was to have served in the U.S. Navy. I got to tell you also more importantly he was proud of the fact that he became an American Citizen.

I drove over to my sister's house and told her the story about the medals and that they had arrived. I took them out of the box and showed her and admittedly cried feeling the same way I did knowing that dad would have been proud as hell to have had those medals on the wall in the apartment.

Dad didn't achieve much in the material world or become rich monetarily but he gained dignity and respect for himself and the family.... My father was a people person. He loved the family life. He loved to go visiting with family and friends. He loved the Holidays especially the Christmas season. He was a traditionalist. When I was maybe 5 or 6 years old I remember he would not get a Christmas Tree until Christmas Eve. He would buy the biggest tree he could find.

The tree would be so big that he would have to cut the top to fit it in the parlor when he stood it up in the tree stand.

He would always make a joke and say "Oh well we have to cut a hole in the ceiling again this year." Of course as a little guy I would believe that remark and I was so happy that he didn't make a hole and that he would cut the tree top instead—*what a dopey little kid I was at times.*

As a family we had the best time decorating the tree. Mom would make us hot chocolate as we strung on the lights and then go crazy throwing the silver tinsel on the branches. Dad would wait until the end and then get a ladder and place the Angel on the top of the tree. He kept that tree up almost until Easter.

My father was a hard driven hard working person. He wasn't your typical "Let's go for a catch in the yard" type of father. But a father that knew right and wrong and knew how to teach and express "to be a good person" in life. Not by words but by expression, feelings and a good heart of love!

Dad was not much of the disciplinarian in the family. He sort of left that up to my mother who kept us in line for sure.

Me & Roberta walking down the aisle at St. Joseph Church
Al & Francis Iscaro's Wedding

My Mother Esther Iscaro Nardone

Uncle Louie

Mom&Dad Wedding Annv

Italian mothers never threw a baseball in their life, BUT . . .

They can nail you in the head with a slipper thrown from the kitchen while you are in the living room!

Slipper

Like I said prior my mom was the disciplinarian in the family (although my sister was a close second—I don't mean that in a bad sense she was the center of our family connection). My mother would preach cleanliness for yourself and your living space and belonging's. She would always say "Make sure you always wear clean underwear in case of an accident and something happens to you." But as life went on, we all found out just about every mother said that!

Mom surely kept us all in line. She held no punches (although she would take a few swipes here and there at us.)

Mom had it rough. By being the strong one in the family she basically guided my father because of his heavy Italian accent and at times when he would find it difficult communicating with people. If they didn't speak Italian he had a little bit of a hard time expressing and communicating with people that weren't of the Italian language. Mom also had to deal with complications of her first child (My brother was born legally blind with epilepsy and a brain deficiency.) It was not very easy to handle your first child with issues like my brother had and what made matters even more difficult World War II broke out and my father went on to serve in the U.S. Navy as mentioned in the prior section of the book. So my mom had to raise and handle the problems of my brother and of course have a roof over her head and food on the table. Because of the close nit proximity of the family and her good friend Rose Circelli she like a lot of ladies in "West" New Rochelle dealt with the chore of being a single parent while the father was off to war.

When my father returned home from war and my sister Diane was born mom always worked as a second income for the family. Basically her profession was a cashier. She worked in supermarkets but as long as I remember she worked many years for Daylight Meateria on Main St. in New Rochelle and then Pelham Meateria on 5th Ave in the Village of Pelham—NY.

Through out all those years she maintained the family. *And* when I say the family I mean raising us to learn family values, respect for your neighbors, friends and *all* people. She taught us how to act among the family—Our manners—sit up, eat properly, when to be heard, when to be seen and by and large "Treat people the way you wish to be treated."—It's as easy and simple as that!

I found coming from the "West End" of New Rochelle all mother's—father's instilled that protocol of family life and respect to their children. That is just one of the reasons coming from the "West" was a special place to be raised in the 50's, 60's & 70's.

My mom did everything that can possibly be done to help my brother maintain, learn, survive and grow up from an adolescent to an adult that can function in a society on his own. Medically my brother needed to be taken care of professionally and physically to function under his adverse well being. You have to remember back in the 50's-60's it was no where the profession of training, medication and assistance from the medical field, schools and government as there is now not to mention monetary value of cost.

As the youngest in her family my mother came to the USA at a very early age. My mom attended the New Rochelle School System. She left New Rochelle High School which was at the time Albert Leonard School (now New Rochelle City Hall) at an early age to go to work for an added family income.

She loved America always stressing to the family and my father to learn the language & the culture. She spoke the Italian language but made sure she spoke English most of the time.

Mom would converse with my father in Italian when us kids were not supposed to know what they were speaking about.

Unfortunately, mom and dad never taught us kids the Italian language. What a shame it would have been a great asset to learn the language.

My mother's side of the family was my Uncle Mike Iscaro (he was the Yankee Fan), Uncle Joe Iscaro (he was the Golfer in the family), Uncle Louis "Louie" Iscaro (he was the flamboyant dancer who ended up moving to Arizona), my Aunt Mary who married Joseph Mandracchia who was from New Rochelle and related to "Millie's Grocery Store on Union Ave and my Aunt Carmella who married Alex Morelli who was from Yonkers and took his family to be raised there.

My grandmother (moms mother) was a "Pastore." and the family was from the Naples area of Italy as well as my dad's family.

Mom—Me & Brother Anthony

Mom & Me

Dad—Sis Diane & Me

Godmother Francis Iscaro Brother Anthony & Me

Grand-Mother "Pastore"

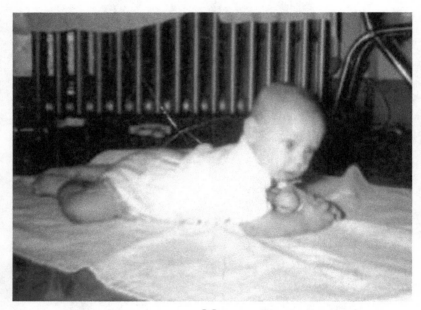

Me

My Brother Anthony Nardone Jr,

Son's Pix

At birth my brother Anthony was born legally blind as I mentioned in the previous chapter with epilepsy and what they called at that time a "Mental Deficiency"—What happened was, at least how I remember it. While growing up it was never discussed by my parents or told to me what actually did happened.

At birth, my mother was having problems giving birth with my brother and the doctors used some sort of "prongs" (that apparently back in the 40's was a procedure) and my brother's skull was injured somehow in the process when he was delivered by the doctors. Back then their was nothing known as law suits!

My brother was no dummy by any means of the imagination. Yes, he had a handicap both physically and mentally. But he managed to live life to the fullest and the best that he can until his death at the tender age of 53 years old.

He loved to eat, he loved music and he loved to GO!

What do I mean by GO? As I remember it (because my brother was 8 years older then me) as a teenager and a young man he would "hang" with the guys and gals in the neighborhood. His nickname was "Butch" and the guys would love having him around as they watched him closely.

Like I said prior, back in the 50's and early 60's they didn't have the education, schools, resources, medication or just the know how to teach or properly give the right assistance and care to someone like my brother. My family did have him attend the school system. First starting out in St. Joseph Catholic School on 6th St. But forget that, the nuns with all do respect had no system for that type of student so that was out. He did attend the Jewish Guild for the Blind in the Bronx. But even the New Rochelle Public School System just was not equipped with the proper education for people like my brother.

I remember seeing pictures of my brother in school and they would be sitting in the basement of the school. It was difficult for my brother to read because of his eye sight. It was difficult for him to comprehend because he had a terrible case of epilepsy that took many years of new medication for it to be controlled. The bottom line is it was never really under control. I can't tell you how many times my brother ended up in a hospital by having a seizure. He probably was in every hospital in the Bronx, Brooklyn and lower Westchester. It sounds like a joke but it sure wasn't when the telephone rang at home. My mother prayed to St. Jude constantly that God would watch over him hoping he would not fall under a train or get hit by a car or whatever! I say a train because my brother had a talent to travel every train and subway in the New York area. Don't ask me how, he just knew how to get from Westchester County to Staten Island to Brooklyn to the Bronx like the back of his hand. It was just amazing. My mother was always bewildered of the fact he can go anywhere. But yes, there were many phone calls from all over that my brother had a seizure and he was in the hospital.

My brother studied on his own as well. He self taught himself a lot. They had what they called "Talking Books"—Big LP records would come in this hard case via the US mail. They were stories and they were study guides about some sort of education process, subject and short story novels. My brother studied and learned brail on his own. In fact he would ask me to help him. As an 8 year old I was helping him learn brail and in the interim I learned it myself. I would close my eyes and read brail. I remember we had the little pointer to punch holes when writing. The touch and the feeling was the important part of learning brail with the letters and numbers. Once you get that down the reading was simple.

The radio was a big part of my brother's life. It was great therapy for him. He would listen day and night. He would lie n bed (we shared the same room) at night and listen to talk shows. During the day it was music. I now know how and why I am a huge radio person, talk show and music guy. Inspired by my brother's ability, knowledge and interest of the radio air waves. In fact to this day when I listen to one of my recorded music or talk shows. I do not hear my voice. I hear the sound of my brother's voice hosting that show. It's freaky but I am very happy knowing spiritually it is him talking through me or from me watching and listening to the show. I thank my brother for giving me that interest. I didn't know it back then. But as I got into hosting a radio show I found that inspired ability and interest past down from my brother to me.

My father built this little table with door knobs. My brother would set up the table along with side two turn tables and for hours imagine he was on the radio and on the air hosting a radio show. Like I said it was very therapeutic for him and the family as well that it occupied his body, mind & soul. He even gave himself a DJ name and radio call letters. Known as DJ "Anthony Michael"—His radio station was WAMN.

My brother was the cleanest and neatest person I ever met. I'm telling you every draw in the dresser was neat and stacked very nice. The closet (on his side of the room) was like an army soldier's locker. Nothing out of order or place and everything hanging loosely and neat. His clothes, pants and jackets were always pressed and cleaned like they just came out of the box or wrapper. He always wore a tie no matter were he went. He never did what I would do and that is taking off my shoes, shirt or pants and lay it on the chair or on the bed. Heaven for bid!

That is one trait I wish I had picked up from him and that was to be neat and tidy. But it never happened. Living alone these days I do get a little messy. I do admit it.

I can tell you one trait that my brother taught me and that is to shave without looking in a mirror. Feel and swipe was his motto until the face was smooth. To this day I stand in the shower and feel and swipe. No I never cut myself, well maybe once in awhile.

My sister (God Bless her) took good care of my brother (me I did the best I can as a young kid). While my mother was at work. My sister cleaned, washed and pressed my brothers clothes. She cooked for him (and me too) and made sure he always took his pills/medication. But what is so vivid in my mind from as long as I remember going back to when I was about 5-6 years old "The Crash" (as I called it), the thump of my brother falling from a epilepsy seizure.

My sister was great attending to his needs making sure he didn't injure himself more doing what you had to do until he came out of his seizure. The seizures at times would last 15-30 minutes before he was back on his feet. At times he would have 2 in a row.

There were times my sister was not at home and I would be the one responding. I would be in a deep sleep and when I heard that crash I knew it was my brother having a seizure. I would automatically jump out of bed to attend to him not knowing how bad it would be. He had a terrible case of epilepsy and like I said it took many years before it was under control. I still can remember as a youngster when the police, ambulance would have to respond because he wouldn't come out of the seizures. Back then they had a doctor on the ambulance and he even couldn't get my brother to come out of a seizure at times. They would work on him in my room and it looked like a scene out of a movie, like some sort of exorcism going on. Not a good site for a young kid to see his brother in such need.

One thing never discussed to me as a kid at least (although I heard a few times my mother telling family & friends) was the money spent for my brother for special schools and medication. She was never resentful of what life was like for her as a family. But she mentioned a few times about the house right next door to Columbus Elementary School on Washington Ave opposite Fifth St. across from St. Joseph Church that was for sale for $2500.00 to be exact. My parents just couldn't afford it financially and would have liked to have purchased it. It was a small house but had a huge long backyard enough to have a patio—play in and for dad to have a nice garden for tomato's and peppers. But it just couldn't be done with the expense of my brother's needs and a mortgage and up keep of a house.

My mother always believed that life could always be a lot worse and that there are a lot more people worse off then her and her family.

My Sister Diane Nardone Celenza

Bro&Sis

Long before "Lady Di" was crowned in England. It was only fitting that my sister was named Diane. On my mothers side my sister was the only female born in the Iscaro family while all my Uncle's and Aunt's had boys! She was, as I was told a princess at heart. As she was growing up in her teens and twenties to be a very beautiful woman. Of course today she still is beautiful and a princess and as I run into people from years ago they always ask me first about my sister and how they all remark and say the same thing. "Is she still as pretty as she was when she was young"? Of course I would say "YES"

My sister for all case and point raised myself and my brother as I mentioned in previous sections of this book. As the middle child she had the burden of cleaning, cooking and watching both me and my brother as both my parents went to work.

She handled all my brother's problems very well by making sure he would take his medication and as I mentioned his epileptic seizures. She would feed both of us for the better part of breakfast and lunch. She would iron clothes for the family, clean, vacuum and even start dinner so when my father and mother got home from work it would be pretty well be ready to be served.... My mother would do a lot of preparation of the cooking on weekends for the week and freeze most of it. She would then take it out in the morning as she left for work to defrost and by the afternoon my sister would then start to cook it so by time everyone got home it was ready for all of us to sit down and have dinner as a family.....I do remember the times for whatever reason mom & dad were not home and their was spinach or some green on the plate that I didn't like. My sister was tough on me. I would have to eat most of it before she let me off the table. I didn't realize it then. But mom & dad worked hard for all of us and my sister was not going to have me be a picky eater and waste food.

Diane has greenish eyes and always had light brown or blondish hair. Kind of perfect in size, not tall, not to petit and always in proportion body wise.

My sister got married young to Frederick Celenza. He was known by his friends as (yes, you guessed it) "Tony"—Tony was from the Fordham Road section of the Bronx. A very bright minded person who attended a Catholic Education. Starting with Saint Martin of Tours elementary School, then on to Cardinal Hayes High School and then on to Iona College where he received his under graduate and masters degree's.

They met while Tony was working as a part time college student where my mother worked "Daylight Meateria." I even worked there while I was attending Junior and Senior High School cutting cold cut meats at the deli counter.

Daylight Meateria was located on Main Street just next door to the old Caruso's Music Store and directly across the street from the old RKO Proctor Movie Theater. (I think the "Little Mexican Café" is now in it's place).

Anyway, back around 1965, Tony asked my mother if she would mind if he asked my sister out on a date. By 1967 they where married and purchased their first house in the Bronx and had their first child in 1969. They have three children, Two girls, Christine and Stephanie and the third child named Paul.

They eventually sold the house in the Bronx and purchased a house in the north end of New Rochelle, NY.

Although my sister got married young, for years I remember she still came over to our apartment on Fifth St and helped my mother by cleaning and cooking while my parents were at work.

My sister is very much of a family person and I guess what you would call a home bound type person. She dedicated her life to being a great mother by caring, love and keeping a rightful eye on the kids and the house. She worked very hard doing motherly things like cleaning, washing and ironing clothes, shopping for the house, yard work etc etc. She kept herself in good shape and took care of herself by going to the beauty parlor but that was about it. She never went shopping on clothing excursions and run to the mall just to shop. It was always a need or for the family when it came to shopping.

Before she would settle down to relax and read the newspaper, it was always Tony, the kids, the house, the dog and herself. Something I think my mom instilled in her. A special gift of "love" for family & friends.

Again, part of being brought in the "West End" of New Rochelle, NY Caring for Family & friends.

I'll always remember, when I was about 8 or 9 year's old and in the afternoon's when "American Bandstand" would come on the TV my sister would make me dance with her so she could practice her jitter bug or whatever dance she was trying to learn...

I'll remember sitting at the table with my spinach in front of me pouting that she wouldn't let me go play....*But now in a good way!* I'll remember all the great Holiday's....I'll remember when she took me along to Hudson Park Beach in the summer with her friends! I'll remember you singing to DION and collecting all the 16 Magazines' of the 60's pop stars....I'll remember you giving me your white roller skates and dying them black for me to use at the Boys Club skating nights....I'll remember the terrific summer's in Atlantic City.

Thank You Sis there is so much to Remember!

CHAPTER (5)

"The Fifth Street Neighbors"

Viccaro's Bar & Restaurant – 1952
Left to Right: Front Row: John Viccaro – Lenny Viccaro
Back Row: John Viccaro – Frankie Viccaro – Peter Viccaro
Rosemarie Viccaro – Frankie Viccaro Jr.

Viccaro's Rest

When we moved from the corner of Seventh St. & Union Ave around 1956 from the Immediato apartment building to 9 Fifth St. owned by the Carpenzano family I was 5 years old and in the kindergarten at Columbus Elementary School up on Washington Ave across from St. Joseph Church. As a kid I use to say "Mom how come Columbus School is on Washington Ave?—Why not call it Washington School?"—Well actually there was a Washington School up on the beginning of Union Ave which is now a senior citizens building. So of course my question was why then wasn't Washington School called Columbus and Columbus called Washington?....*Still waiting for the answer.*

My two closest friends were Danny Costa who lived across the street at 4 Fifth St. and Mauro Viccaro II who lived on the third floor above Viccaro's Pizza Parlor.

Next door to us was the Rainone family consisting of George Sr. the Father, Peggy the Mother, Margret the Daughter, George Jr. the Son and Mr. Rainone, George Sr's Father.

Mr. Rainone (Father/Grandfather) was, as I remember him an elderly man that was strong as a bull. He walked with a cane, smoked a pipe but worked like a mule. Always doing something around the house.

In the warm months Mr. Rainone would sit on the green park bench in front of the house by 5am. He then would take care of his chores. Anything from painting his wrought iron fence that he took so much pride in to sweeping the sidewalk and yard.

Mr. Rainone would get so mad at us kids if a ball went in his lovely grass pasture lawn that separated my house where I lived and his house. He had a pool of gold fish about 6'x6' right in his green lawn. Danny and I would have to wait until he went inside or wait later that evening to get the ball when it went in the yard. But if he caught us he would give out a huge yell at us then wave his cane which scared the hell out of us kids.

George Sr. was another hard working guy. He was a landscaper that worked 5 days a week and on Sunday morning's I would always wake up to the sound of him sharpening his lawn mowers and equipment on the revolving grinder. He would sharpen his hedge cutters and take the blades off his lawnmowers and sharpen them one by one. My window was in the back of the apartment so I would get a kick out of just looking out the window and watch him clean all his trucks and machine's. By noon he was done and the afternoon was for him to relax with the family.

In the winter months he turned to plowing snow.

George would donate his time and took care of the grounds around St. Joseph's School and Church. The bushes and grass were always cut trim. I just remember how green everything was. It was so immaculate.

George had a 4 car garage and to the left of it was his collie dog "Rusty's" doghouse with a fenced in yard and plenty of room for the dog to roam. In the winter and bad weather "Rusty" would roam in the cellar section of the house.

Grandpa George Rainone sitting on the bench on 5th St

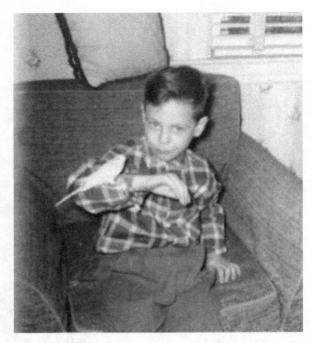

Bird Pix & 5th St Porch

On top of the garage was a double decker pigeon coop. The coop was owned and operated by Jimmy Circelli and a very nice guy named Chucky (I don't remember his last name but I do remember that he didn't live in the "West" (Jimmy lived on 6th St.) and drove a 1956 Plymouth and worked for the 7-up Bottling company in New Rochelle.) In fact Chucky owned a 16' motor boat that he docked at Hudson Park and he would take myself and Mauro out to go water skiing down on the creek by Co-op City. The water was clean then and very calm. Great for skiing.

As kids myself and Mauro loved Pigeon's. We would sit in the yard and watch for hours as they trained for racing, flew and fed the birds. Sunday was race day. What an exciting event that was to watch. Rain or shine. It was great. First of all Saturday evening the birds that you entered in the race would have to be banded (a little rubber band placed on the birds leg that would be taken off when returned to the coop from their destination of the race.) Then at the pigeon club by 8th St. there would be a big truck and all the pigeons would be placed in crates and on the truck. The driver then would drive all night to the destination to let them out for the race. It could be a three hundred mile race, five hundred mile race etc.

You had to know your birds. Things like which bird had more endurance for shorter or longer races. Which birds flew better in the wind or rain. I will never forget my Ball Headed Blue Bar pigeon. (A white headed bird with two stripes on his wings. He was terrible flying in beautiful weather. But give it some inclement weather and he would sore like an eagle always placing among the leaders.

There were so many type of races and of course money was always a factor to win. The name of the coop owned by Jimmy and Chucky was called "St. Joseph Loft."

Jimmy Circelli was a master carpenter and had his own business so you can imagine that the pigeon coop was in the very best of shape.

Jimmy and Chucky eventually allowed Mauro and myself to come up the coop. It was exciting as we entered the gate where the dog was and then climb up the first iron ladder to the roof of the garage. There it was the first coop of pigeons. Basically the birds that were older or mating were housed in that section.

Me and Mauro helped keep the coop clean by scrapping and shoveling the bird droppings. If you didn't pick up the droppings early it would get hard as cement and it took a lot of work to scrape it up.

It was very important to keep the coop clean. If not you will have lots of problems with disease, pigeons getting sick, lice on their wings or even yourself exposed to something nasty!

The next ladder was cemented in to the building of the coop and it was straight up like a navy ship ladder that went about ten feet up in the air. Once at the top you had to climb over the little wall. So now your about 30 feet above the ground. A little frightening as a kid until you got used to looking down.... But great for bird watching and for racing. Very accessible for the pigeons to see when coming in for a landing in the race because time is of the essence.

It was such fun flying the birds and training them to land quickly to return inside the coop. We would have these fan tail white birds that you threw up in the air that didn't fly away. They would just fly to the landing perch area so to attract the pigeons above flying and they would see the white tail birds and get a "birds eye" view of landing on the coop perch to enter inside. We also had these long bamboo poles that when the pigeon landed on the perch we would guide them with these poles to quickly get the bird to enter through the gates so they return inside the coop without hesitation. That procedure was very important when racing so to record fast times.

To record a pigeon on race day. Each coop had a little wooden box with a clock in it. When the bird returned and entered the coop the little rubber band was immediately taken off his leg placed in a capsule and clocked inside the wooden clock box. It worked something like the old security watchman checking different sections of the building and there was a key at different locations to record the time of checking a certain destination.

When most of the birds returned home the members would then go to the club and the judges would open all the boxes to record the times of the pigeons in the race. That is how the winners were determined. A great hobby that took up a lot of time and work. But enjoyable and at times profitable.

Peggy Rainone was a nice lady. Tall and slender that loved sitting in front of the house. She was one of the few ladies on the block that drove a car. I remember she always had a station wagon. I'll never forget the time while in the streets with other kids on the block I turned to run down the street, I took one step and I ran right into an iron street sign pole. BAM!...I saw stars and my forehead was bleeding like crazy. Peggy immediately came running over and placed a wash cloth over the huge cut on my forehead just above my left eye. She then drove me to the New Rochelle Hospital Emergency Room for stitches.... I don't know if I ever really thanked Peggy. So now I say "Thank You Peg" for assisting me with my accident.

Next to the Rainone's was the Garito family. They lived in a white stucco house. Their was Frank Sr. (the Father), Rose (the Mother who was a Pastore by maiden name and related to my mother's side), Frank Jr., Steven and little Roellen and the Grandparents.

Frank Sr. owned a demolition construction company. He was a tall handsome man that people said he resembled Dean Martin.

Frank got involved with politics in New Rochelle. First becoming a district leader and then a run for the Office of the Mayor of New Rochelle in which he was successful in winning and became a popular Elected Official that was loved by all New Rochelle residents especially Fifth St. Neighbors and the Italians from the "West End".

Across the street was another Viccaro Family. Peter the father who was the chef for "Viccaro's Pizza Parlor"

—Louise the mother, Virginia, Mauro III and then Peter who we called Petey.

Next door to the Viccaro's were the DiPippo family. Toni-Ann live their. I remember her as this pretty blond that I always had a crush on. She was friends with Virginia Viccaro. In the same house as the DiPippo's lived the Chipper and John Chimento Family.

Down the block on the corner of Fifth St & Lafayette Ave (1 Fifth St) lived Donald Tedesco, his brother and family. Donald I believe went on to start the "Relig" program in New Rochelle.

Across the street from me was Peter and Camille Spadaro with their son Pete and daughter Donna. Three houses just past the Garito's lived John and Camille Coppolla with their daughters Fran and her sister along with their sons Tony and John.

Camille before she was married lived in the apartment above us at 9 Fifth St. We lived on the second floor and the "Claps" family lived on the third floor. There were the parents Mary and John. Camille the daughter and her brother Frank always known in the neighborhood as "Frankie Claps."

John the father was a master mechanic who had a business in the garage of someone's house on Fourth St. He walked with a limp as I remember. I never knew exactly why he and his brother "Popeye" had problems with their legs. But John was a great guy. He used to drive my mother to work on Main St. four times a week to Daylight Meateria.

Their son Frank was four years older then me, a sports fanatic and went to school with my sister. Frankie loved all sports but baseball was his first love. He never walked anywhere he would always run to where he was going. Frankie went to college at the University of Miami and unfortunately passed away at a very young age. I remember it was so sad for the neighborhood because Frankie was so liked. I remember when growing up Frankie never combed his hair, he just always wanted it messed up for whatever reason. Then one day Frankie returned from college and he was all dressed up and his hair was slicked back combed so neatly. Everyone on the block was amazed. I remember saying "Hey Frankie you look different" and Frankie said laughing "Get used to it kid." But Frankie was a really nice guy. Always pleasant, polite to my parents and respectful to my brother and sister.

Camille and along with her mom Mary were opera singers. First let me tell you they were maybe five feet tall. Small in stature but man can they belt out opera tunes. Weekends was when they rehearsed their voices. Every Saturday was 7am till the afternoon. I was out of the house by 7:30am on Saturday's so it didn't bother my sleep.

But it did have an effect on the rest of the household including my cousin on the first floor. On Sunday they started singing about 9am. They would sing as loud as they can to train their voices. After awhile it didn't bother anyone anymore, people just got used to it and slept right through it. In fact you really appreciated the bellowing amazing sound these two little ladies were able to create. To this day Camille I believe is still involved with the New Rochelle Opera. Camille and her mom Mary where also tremendous nice people.

Next door to the Coppolla's lived Mary and Frank Datillo. They lived at 23 Fifth St. with their kids Joseph, Frank, Cathy, Susan and Fran. I always remember them or at least the kids when they were young always hanging in their yard playing among themselves. They never really came out onto the street to play kickball or other games with the rest of the kids. But as they got to be teens they then started hanging out with the people of the neighborhood. Frannie as I call her really became a community activist. With all her years of working as a waitress she got to know everyone in New Rochelle and the politicians and civic groups always asked for her help and she was there in between being a mother and working so many late hours.

Up on the corner of Fifth St. and Union Ave in the stucco house just across the street from St. Joseph Convent and next door to Viccaro's Restaurant was the Rosita Family. Their entrance to their apartment was on Union Ave but their yard was on Fifth St. There was Rocky the father, Vinci the mother and their two children Steven and Vivian. Rocky worked for the water company for many years. His wife Vinci was a lovely lady. Always so nice and always allowed all of us kids to just hang in the yard with them and their two kids Steven and Vivian. I remember when Vivian was born. It was the first baby I ever held in my arms. I was so nervous but Vinci said "don't worry it's OK."

In their yard they had a tremendous grape vine that was a covering over their patio. It completely covered the iron pipes and kept out the sun and weather element. Great for sitting underneath during the hot summer months or the nice cool summer evenings. It was pretty neat just picking the grapes, squeezing them into our mouth.

On the first floor of the house where I lived was my cousin Al Iscaro known to family as "Bunky" (Don't ask me why.) He was married to my Godmother Francis Guida Iscaro. They had two boys Michael and John along with their daughter Lisa. Cousin Bunky loved big cars and loved to keep them clean and shiny. Bunky and my father would see who could shine their car the shiniest. Every weekend cleaning and shinning their cars. Bunky also loved opera and liked to play golf. He had various jobs as I remember. I remember him in the early 60's selling door to door insurance. Then he was a supermarket manager. Then along with his brother in law they bought a grocery business on Coligni and Horton Ave. A predominately black neighborhood along with factories in the area. They had the business for about 15 years and did very well there.

My Godmother Francis was a very nice lady. Very religious. I remember Francis, her sister and brother along with their kids were all so good looking. The whole family was handsome and pretty! Her family lived up on Washington Ave by the Ritacco gas station. Francis would always say how she once had a date with the famed singer Jerry Vale and make jokes how she should of stayed with him. Fran drove a black Ford Falcon car. I'll never forget that car. I believe it was a 1961. She just loved driving that car everywhere. She was a great cook too. Great meatballs! But I do remember she gave me my first "T.V. Dinner."

Cousin Michael was a cool little kid, when he was young around 9 years old to 12 he was always getting into trouble. Nothing big, just little mischievous things. Just a kid having fun in the neighborhood. But he grew up to be a nice respectful person. Michael got married and moved to Tennessee. Now his brother John on the other hand was quite and loved sports. A very bright kid and a smart kid who always did the right thing. Never got in trouble. He worked with the church, went to college, got married. Just a serious honest person. People said he should have been a priest. Just a good kid. John still lives in New Rochelle with his wife Theresa who is from Greenwich Connecticut. My cousin Lisa as I remember her was a little doll. Bunky just loved his little girl. She was so pretty and dainty. Francis always dressed her up like a little Barbie Doll. She like John, was quite. Lisa got married and lives up in Dutchess County.

Bunky has two brothers Anthony and Michael. Anthony who is about 11 years older then me moved to Florida with his wife Patricia before I really got to know them. Michael the youngest of the three eventually moved down south but while I was growing up he lived on Fifth Ave in New Rochelle with Uncle Mike and Aunt Mary Iscaro. My Uncle Mike always called me "McDougal" after the Yankees baseball player Gil McDougal of the 60's. The nickname started to stick with me but mom quickly put a stop to that for whatever reason!

Uncle Mike was my mother's older brother. I always enjoyed when we went to Fifth Ave to visit. They had their own house with this little above ground pool. Cousin Michael would let me sleep over and hang with him and his friends. Michael was a few years older. So when I was 11 years old he was like 15. At that time it felt like such a huge age difference. Anyway he would take me along with his friends to hike in the woods and fish down at Pinebrook Lake.

My cousin Anthony and Pat, like I said prior, moved to Florida while I was still young and I didn't really get to know them. But when I was

20 years old and went to Florida is when I did get to know both of them very well. I was there for a year in 1971 and Anthony and Pat treated me like I was Anthony's younger brother. Pat opened her doors to me, fed me and watch out for me everyday. She was always giving me advice and introducing me to the girls. She is great! Anthony let me use his car and brought me all over the place wherever they went. They never stayed home. If they weren't entertaining they were going to someone's house for dinner, coffee or drinks. Anthony became a successful business man who had two children Anthony Jr. and Michelle. To this day Michelle is the prettiest girl I have ever seen! You have to see her to believe me.

Anthony Jr. became a tremendous athlete. Ran like a deer. He played football before an injury changed his career.

Back to the neighborhood. My Grandmother Iscaro lived in the red flat across the street from St. Joseph Church on Fifth St. just before Washington Ave. When I was younger she lived on St. John's Place just off Fourth St.

In the same red flat lived Elvin Brown. His mother Mrs. Brown still lives there alone with about 7 rooms for herself.

I remember Elvin from Columbus School. He was great in playing kickball. When we were in the 6th grade and played behind the school during lunch Elvin would kick the ball up in the old fire escape and also into the roof where they would burn the coal to heat the school.

Bobby Gaita lived in that red flat also. Bobby was a great guy. He passed away a couple of years ago. Bobby was my sister's age, he went into the Marines and served our country. I remember when he came home.

He was still a nice guy but something about Bobby was a little different. Bobby worked many years in the Post Office. Bobby was a pretty good athlete and softball player. He was small in physique but had a huge heart of love for his Family, Friends, "The West" and his Country and believe me was tough as nails!

On Union Ave between Fifth St. and Fourth St. across from the "Pool Room" and next door to the Della Donna Family in the 4 story apartment building lived Grandpa & Grandma Nardone. My dad would take me their to visit them when I was very young. I remember they lived on the top floor and I was amazed how I can look down onto Union Ave and see behind the Nuns Convent and see everyone going into the pool room. But then Grandma died and grandpa went to live with Aunt Rita across the street above the pool room. I remember my Grandmother making ravioli the size of the dish. She would give you just one huge ravioli. I don't remember too much about grandma except her name was Lucia and the big ravioli too!

On the corner of Fifth St. and Union Ave, diagonally across from "Popeye's" and St. Joseph Convent, was this store front that years ago was a grocery store that was then turned into an apartment. They had these curtains hanging up to cover the large glass store type windows. Anyway, the Frederick's family lived there. I remember Larry (who I played Little League with on the team named the "Jets." Also in the family were Raymond, Joe, Michael and Paul (all brothers). I believe there mother's name was Pauline. They were all very nice people as I remember them. Raymond hung out with us a lot in the neighborhood. Whatever happened to all of them—I just don't know. Maybe I can find them on Face book!

Getting back to Viccaro's Pizza Parlor on Union Ave between Fifth St and Sixth St. Their was no other restaurant like it. People came from all over to Viccaro's. As I mentioned earlier in the book the Pizza was the Best!—The Hero's were the best. I know because all the ingredients they used were home grown from the garden in their rear yard. I would help Mauro dig the dirt in the spring. They had two separate gardens with a red brick walkway down the middle. Each year Mauro's grandfather would use one side and then leave the other side free. I was told that's the way it works to have a good garden. To keep it fresh you should not use the dirt year after year. Mauro's grandfather would grow tomatoes of course, red and green peppers, zucchini, eggplant, basil and all the vegetables for the restaurant.

At the end of the summer they would jar the tomatoes for future gravy for the pasta and pizza for the winter months.

When you first walk into Viccaro's Restaurant they had a huge couch like booth along the main window and then chairs and tables.

The bar was next door to the restaurant. It wasn't the kind of bar you would go and have a drink while waiting for a table. It was basically a neighborhood bar.

When the customers ordered a drink from the waiter there was this little window that connected the restaurant and the bar which was separated by two sliding little doors which had a ledge. The bartender would slide the doors open and place the drinks on the ledge.

Customers loved those sliding doors. *A trademark of Viccaro's.*

As I mentioned in chapter 4 the bar wasn't exactly the classiest lounge in the world. As I said it certainly had all the "custom" of the neighborhood. The bar was filled with men smoking heavy and playing cards, drinking $10 cents beers, and talking about if the Mick hit another homer!

When you ordered a take out pizza you would walk in the bar to pick it up. Of course we knew everyone in the bar and they would be courteous and say "How's your mom—dad & family?" If you had to wait a couple of minutes someone would always yell "give the kid a soda."

Mauro the III (who lived on Fifth St) worked with his father all the time. You would always see Mauro running back and forth from the restaurant to his house with his white apron. George Rainone said he was always bringing home money so not to leave a lot of cash in the restaurant. *Who knows but Mauro*—I'll ask him next time I see him.... Mauro the III became a very good cook and it was too bad he didn't carry on the tradition of the restaurant when it eventually closed. But I guess he would have had to buy out all the brother's and whoever else in the Viccaro family that had a piece of the restaurant. What a sad day that was. First the restaurant closed and then eventually the bar closed. As I mentioned people came from miles around to eat at Viccaro's. On a Friday night cars would be parked all over the place and the neighborhood would go nuts because there were no parking spaces on the streets from 4pm till 11pm.

Another good little pizza parlor was on the corner of Fourth St. and St. John's Place. "Johnnie's Kitchen"—Which became Giovanni's Italian Restaurant on Main St. down the block from the old library opposite the corner of Beechwood Ave. It didn't have the magnitude of Viccaro's but they made a very tasty pizza pie.

My dad loved going to Giovanni's and I did also because they made ravioli like my grandmother did. One big huge ravioli that filled the whole plate. It was sooooo good.

Now it is Juliano's Catering Hall. But I sure do miss Giovanni's food along with a Viccaro's Sausage & Peppers Hero!!!!

On the corner of Fifth St. and Union was "Popeye's" candy store—if you wish to call it that! It was known in the neighborhood as one of those places you handed someone a little piece of paper with maybe a dime or

$35 cents wrapped in it. But he did have penny candy and us kids did buy our baseball cards there.

Popeye was the brother of John Claps (who lived on the third floor of 9 Fifth St just above us) as I mentioned in prior chapters. Popeye was small in height and like John had some sort of disability and walked with a huge limp. But Popeye loved baseball and would tell us kids stories about the Yankees of the 50's and early 60's.

Down the block where Fifth St. met Lafayette Ave were the Signorelli Family, Joe & Carol Barone, Sal Palazzo and Family with Richard and Jackie, Leno Gianotti, Allen Vaccaro, Joanne Signorelli was my age (unfortunately she died young also) her father Ralph was a small guy but he would scare the heck out of me, Mauro & Danny. Their property backed up onto the railroad tracks. As I mentioned prior in the book myself, Danny and Mauro would always play along the tracks. It was real cool hang-in down on the tracks for some crazy reason. I guess the excitement of a train coming and we would have to get out of the way. We would place pennies on the tracks (had to be new shiny pennies) and have them flatten out then go home and drive a small nail through it and hang them. But we also would place rocks and sticks on the tracks and watch as the train would run them over and get excited to see the rocks and sticks fly all over the place. Sounds crazy but we were kids!

The little cave we found was really neat as we would crawl in there and hide. But again, we never thought if a train rumbled by and somehow the opening of the cave caved-in no one would ever find us! *Like I said we were kids!*

Anyway to get on the tracks we had to slip through the iron fence and Ralph could see us from his yard and he would chase us with his shot gun or at least it looked like a shot gun.

But we still managed after school and during the summer months to slip past Ralph and hang down on the tracks. I got to say, Danny was really the brave one. He would run across to the fourth set of tracks and place pennies on the track. Myself and Mauro really didn't go past the second row of tracks. Danny said the last row of tracks were the fast trains so the penny would flatten better. But anyway we would see the lights above change meaning a train was coming as it rolled around the corner from the train station and it would start to pick up speed. We would yell to Danny to get back here and get off the tracks. Danny would wait till the train appeared in sight and then come running. We used to tell him don't wait so long if you ever tripped you wouldn't make it. But Danny never listened he was a dare devil at heart and always lived on the edge.

We would then send Danny back out to the fourth set of tracks to go collect the pennies for us.

There was this one time Danny scared the shit out of us for real. He fell on the tracks and started to flap his arms and legs and was screaming. Mauro and I thought he got electrocuted. We froze and didn't know what to do, go for help or go get him? But we were afraid we might get electrocuted so we decided to run for help and then the bastard got up laughing like crazy at us. Funny then but as the years went by we didn't realize how real that could have been.....*Like I said we were kids!*

We did a lot of stupid nutty things down on those tracks that Danny, Mauro and myself will always remember! We stopped when investigators came to Columbus School giving lectures about kids hanging down on the tracks....We will leave it at that!

Danny Costa was wild, daring, a thrill seeker and loved a good fight with someone. He didn't care who he fought or how beat up he got he just loved to fight. He would come to school wearing his dungarees under his school pants. After school he would take off his school pants so not to ruin them and hand them to me to hold while he got into his fight. Danny wasn't a bully or anything he just loved to get into some sort of fight for whatever reason. If he lost the fight, he would go back the next day and fight that person again. Danny wasn't that big, maybe 5'7" and not necessarily strong, just sort of scrappy and more of a wrestling type fighter and he kinda liked to grab you in a clutch hole as opposed to punching his fists into someone. I guess that's because he was a big fan of TV wrestling. He never missed watching wrestling on TV with his father who we called "Coach."

When I say Danny was daring and a thrill seeker, well I told you all about our railroad tracks fun but Danny would love to climb trees, jump over fences, over cars, jump from porch to porch anything to be daring and risk his body. Mauro and I would dare him to do things all the time like "Hey Danny bet you can't climb to the top of that tree" and he'd say Oh yea just watch and he would be like a little monkey and scamper from limb to limb. He wasn't trying to impress anyone just loved doing risky things.

One time we said to Danny bet you can't jump from my porch over the walkway over the fence into the grassy knoll. Not thinking that he would do something like that he stood up on the wall (Mauro & I tried to talk him out of this one) and leaped and made it to the grassy knoll. Had he missed he would have fell at least 12' below into the brick walkway or if he didn't clear that wooden green picket fence who knows how hurt he would of got! Not to mention when he landed he had to watch out for the oil pipe coming out of the ground! *Crazy Danny at his Best!*

I remember Danny made these close-pin shooting guns with rubber bands that would shoot matches and of course when you shot these matches it would strike off a match of fire. Mauro and I thought they were real cool. So this one hot summer dry day all three of us are shooting these matches in this open lot besides Danny's backyard. As we shot the matches it would cause these little brush fires and we would stomp it out and use the garden hose to extinguish the little fire. Except this one time we couldn't get the fire out and it spread like crazy! Then we hear this old lady from the apartment building from 6th St. in the back yelling FIRE and called the Fire Department. Danny's mother "Katie" came out of the house yelling at us three especially Danny telling him her famous line "Wait to your father get's home—he is going to give you some shot." By the time "Coach" got home he was so tired from driving and hauling dirt all day from the construction job he could care less what Danny did just give Coach his De Nobili Italian cigar and he was happy.

Danny, Mauro and myself had a lot of good times and memories as kids. In the summer months we were out of the house from 7am until the street lights went on. When the lights went on we would have to check in at home, but as soon as our parents knew we were around the street they would let us hang outside more and anyway people sat in front of their house to the wee hours of the evening's.

Mauro loved shining his 3 speed English Black Racer Bicycle as they called them back then. Danny and I would love to play whiffle-ball early in the morning against the Della-Donna garage facing the Rosita yard. He was always the San Francisco Giants and I would be the NY Yankees of the 1961 Team. In the afternoon we would hike the streets, the tracks or go to Columbus School to play horseshoes and have lemon ice from Sacone's. Nello Amori worked the playground where we would get all our recreation equipment.

In the evening like I mentioned in the prior chapter their was nothing like a good ole game of kickball in the streets or some sort of hide and go seek game. Maybe 3-Flights up with our pink Spaulding ball against the front steps.

Mauro and I would sit on his garage and gaze up at the stars and talk about what the future would be like in space.

On Friday nights we would hang out at Danny's house in the finished basement. Danny had a pool table in the back room but as always it would turn into a wrestling match of us three wrecking the place. The best was when Danny would take us into the work shed and under the work bench were these old black and white old time porno books.

Imagine 10-11 years old getting our first look at naked woman pictures. When we heard noise or footsteps upstairs we would run like hell with our hearts beating thinking of what would happen if we got caught.

The best is when it was time for our neighborhood Good-Humor Ice Cream Truck with "Pete the Good Humor" Ice Cream Man. He came down the block about 8-8:30pm every night without fail. We would all jump on his truck for a ride. We would be hanging on the back, climb on the roof, on the sides and all us kids would be ringing the heck out of the bells. Pete would then sing his famous song to all the kids using all their names. It went something like this:

"Dennis—Dennis is a Friend of Mine—he reminds me of Frankenstein and when he does the Irish Jig he reminds me of Porky Pig!

We would run home to get the money. $35 Cents for my Good Humor Bar on a stick. Pete was an Icon for years in the West End of New Rochelle dressed in his white uniform, hat and bow tie!

Won 2nd Place—500 Mile

Hofkens hen
9061

Won 1st Place

Westchester County Center Pigeon Show—Nov. 17th—1962

My father had given me these old hickory shafted golf clubs that had no leather grips on the them. So this one time while playing in my driveway Mauro and I were hitting rocks with the clubs against the garage. I decided I was going to go back a little further to hit a longer shot of the rocks. *WELL*—Mauro who was in front of me almost had his head taken off by me. What happened was the golf club slipped out of my hand, went flying like a spear straight towards Mauro's head!—*BAM*—it hit Mauro right in the neck and shoulder just missing his head. I can still see that look on his face that he gave me like "What the F—are you doing? Are you crazy!" Of course seeing that Mauro was OK, I laughed and laughed as Mauro left the driveway screaming at me. "Your Nuts"—"Your Nuts" … But it was an accident I was yelling back to Mauro. When we both seen he was OK, I explained it was a accident and apologized and then we both laughed it off together.

I had gotten my own pigeon coop and man was I so excited. Danny, Mauro and myself got the coop from Joe Banana's & Mike Delio if I remember right. So we put the coop on the little red wagon and the three of us wheeled it around the corner up the hill and placed it between the garage and the next door neighbor's house.

Jimmy Circelli gave me a couple of pigeons to get started and then we went to Sacco's grocery store and he then gave me a couple of pigeons and also to get some feed for the birds. But before you know it we were mating pigeon's and raising our own little pigeon coop of birds. Now being a novice at raising pigeons we were a little stupid on how to train them to fly and return to the coop. We did some dumb things like taking a bird or two to my bedroom and letting them fly around the room. We then tried tying a string to the pigeons foot and then letting it go. Yks when the bird took off and then the string ran out—Flop went the bird…*Sorry—We were Kids!*

Jimmy and Chucky almost rang our necks when they found out what we did. By then they started to teach us how to raise pigeons the right way. That's when they started to bring us up on their pigeon coop to help them. *But I have to blame Mauro it was all his idea and how to train a pigeon and have it come back to the coop.*

In my driveway we would have some great basketball games. The driveway was not paved, just some dried up dusty dirt. Our basketball hoop was a wooden bushel that we would get from Sacco's grocery store on the corner of Fourth St. and Union Ave. It was an old peach fruit basket. We would nail it to the garage and by a couple of days it would be hanging and all banged up so we would have to go get another basket from Sacco's.

I don't even know if they sold iron basketball hoops in the stores in the early 60's. But we made the most of it, that's what we had and we had great times doing it in the "West".

Same with a bat & ball. We had one ball and one bat. If that bat cracked we would keep taping it till it fell apart for good. Same with a ball. If the cover came off, we just kept taping over it till there was no more ball left to hit.

In the hot summer day's we would get some adult to un-cap the fire hydrant and cool us off until the fire department came and re-capped it. After happening too many times with the fire hydrant's in the neighborhood the recreation department came up with some sort of sprinkler system at the Columbus School playground. It just wasn't the same. We missed that powerful gush of water coming at us. *Like I said we had our own Niagara Falls!*

As I mentioned prior my sister would take me to Hudson Park Beach. But Danny, Mauro and myself were about 12 years old so we found our way to Wilson Woods Pool in Mount Vernon. We would start out about 8am in the morning because we would make a few stops along the way. First thing we would do is stop at Millie's grocery store on Union Ave directly across the street from Viccaro's Restaurant and buy our bologna sandwich on a Kaiser roll for $25 cents (if you wanted Cheese on it then it was then $35 cents.)

So we then head on down Washington Ave into Pelham. At the bottom of the hill of Washington Ave we made another stop by the old stone protestant church on the corner from the Pelham Train Station. There was always a bunch of pigeons up in the rafters. They were not homing pigeons, they were what you would call "Clinkers"—but from time to time we would see a good looking bird with a band on it's leg that probably got lost in flight during bad weather and what happens they tend to kind of migrate with other pigeons somewhere else and they never make it back to their owners coop. We would try to catch it to see where they were from but we could never because the pigeons had some real nice hide-aways up in those rafters.

We then make our way across 5th Ave in Pelham towards the lake along the Hutchinson River Parkway and make another stop as we talk to whoever was fishing and then go throw rocks in the lake and see how many times we can make them skid along the water before they would sink. We would have our own little contest. The trick was to use nice flat rocks that had a little weight to it but not really heavy and throw it side arm. I think every kid did that sometime in their young life....*You know like Opie did in the beginning of the "Andy Griffith Show"*

Another crazy thing we would do along the way to the pool was while walking if you would a see a used "Lucky Strike" cigarette wrapper on the ground we would step on it and it would allow you to punch the arm of who was next to you. But you had to keep your foot on the wrapper as you hit someone. Sounds nuts but we would to get in some real nice punches in to each other!

After a day at the pool we would do the same thing on our way home. The lake rock throwing, Lucky Strikes punching, the church search for pigeons except Millie's it was time for dinner at home.

Danny and Mauro played the accordion and we couldn't do anything after dinner until they finished practicing at home. They were students at the Carozza Music School. They were pretty good. One time I said let me try so Mauro put the accordion on my chest, strapped me in and showed me a chord with my fingers. I then tried opening the bellow of the accordion and the dam thing just opened all the way and I almost broke it as Mauro had to catch it before it hit the floor. That was the end of my accordion try out!

Danny had a Newspaper Route—It covered Union Ave from 6th St. to 1st St. past the Marciano Bakery & flat. I would help Danny at times. The biggest apartment buildings were on Union Ave with some 5-6 stories of steps to carry up and deliver newspaper's. The "Standard Star" newspaper (in a bundle) was dropped off on the corner of Union & 5th St. We would throw them on the red wagon and try to deliver them as fast as we can so we could get to play some football or baseball depending on the season. It cost $40 cents a week for the newspaper to be delivered for six days and hopefully the customer would give you $50 cents with a $10 cents tip.

On Thursday's Danny would start to collect his delivery money from the customers. He had this little black binder book that sort of looked like a policeman's handy black book that he kept in his back pocket for notes. When the customer paid for the week Danny would make this little X in the square to indicate the customer paid.

The best time to knock on doors was dinner time. Unfortunately you interrupted family dinners but you had no choice. Most of the customers knew it was newspaper collection time and would have the money ready or some would say please come back later or some customers would leave the money on the front mat.

It became a pain at time because some customers would lag behind for 3-4 weeks and then it was a big chunk of money, especially the tip for 4 weeks.

Saturday morning Danny would have to go to the open grassy lot on the corner of Webster Ave and Sickles Ave. (now there are houses there) with all the other kids and meet the Newspaper collection guy who would collect the money from the kids. You would owe a certain amount to him and whatever was left that was your tip money. Danny would also get paid for delivering the newspaper. After that is was lunch money and we would head on over to Joe the butcher for a Sausage & Pepper hero or Mirabella's Grocery for a Italian Cold Cut Sub.

As a young kid I remember when in 1961 John Glenn circled the earth three times. It was such big news in the neighborhood which had everyone saying "wow" imagine that a man in a spaceship going around the world in space—What's Next?—I remember my neighbor from the third floor Mary Claps was so amazed she just kept talking about it to everyone....My mother could care less, she said I still have to go to work in the morning, that money they are spending on spaceships could be spent on us!....*Don't argue with Mom on that one!*

Also as a young kid one of my most saddest and memorable times is when President John F. Kennedy was assassinated in 1963. Everyone who was alive then I'm sure remembers where they were. I was in Isaac. E Young Jr. High School on Pelham Road in 7th grade. I can remember like it was yesterday when the announcement came over the classroom loud speaker during the 7th period and the Principal said we have a very important announcement to make. Please listen carefully. Everyone just looked up and stared at the speaker on the wall above the black chalk board—"President Kennedy while riding in a motorcade in Downtown Dallas, Texas has been shot and is in critical condition at the the local Dallas Hospital." Everyone just looked at each other in amazement and was in shock. Teachers didn't know what to say, they were crying while trying to comfort all the students. They immediately released us from school. Going home that day while walking you can feel the black cloud over everyone. Things seemed so quite and confusing. People walking and talking about what had just happened. Yelling "President Kennedy Shot"!—When we got to Main St. and Centre Ave all the stores had people hobbled around the front doors listening to what was being said on the store radio's.

When I got home I remember putting on the T.V.... Mom made me watch all the events of what was going on.

I watch the funeral with all the military personnel going down Washington D.C.—The lonesome horse with no rider—The casket going down Pennsylvania Ave. Mrs. Kennedy with little Caroline and "John—John: Saluting to his father....It was so sad....

I could remember sitting in our white chair in the living room and watching as the Dallas Police were escorting Lee Harvey Oswald the accused killer/shooter of the President and then all of a sudden "POP" out of no where Jack Ruby jumps in front of Oswald and shoots him with that little 38 snub nose pistol.

I can still see Oswald's face as he crunches in pain grabbing his stomach. Then the bedlam started. Who was grabbing Ruby, who was picking up Oswald to get him to the hospital—all on National T.V.—I remember yelling to my mother "Mom they just shot Oswald"—she came running over saying what is going on in this country!

Some of our other neighbors on Fifth St were Danny's sister's Patty Ann & Toni. Next door was Carl and Angie Guida with there daughter Carol. Toni and Carol were friends with my sister Diane.

Then there was Tony Monteleone who was a vehicle fanatic of keeping his cars sparkling clean. I just remember he was not fond of the fact that us kids played ball in the middle of Fifth Street and heaven for bit a ball came within 10 feet of his vehicle he would be go banana's on us.

Everyone else on the block were elderly and just stayed to themselves. My neighbor next door, I never knew them. They never came outside. *Pretty weird house to be honest as a kid growing up.*

Corner of Washington Ave & Webster Ave
(It was great during Christmas Season)

Saccone's the way it stands today—We remember when it
was a little shack with a Small aluminum window—selling
Lemon Ice for 10 Cents & long pretzels for 2 cents

FORESTER'S CLUB in the 50's

CHAPTER (6)

"The Neighborhood Stores"

Candy Store's	Popeye's—Cannata's—Cooney's—Goose's
Grocery	Millie's Grocery—Immediato Grocery—Sacco's—
	Paolucci's Grocery & Deli—Mirabella's Grocery—
	Amori's Grocery—Guarri's Grocery—Bellontoni's
Pharmacy	Zito's Pharmacy
Shoe Repair	Joe's Shoe Repair
Bread Bakery	Galati's Bakery—West Side Bakery—Marciano's
Bakery	"The Cake Shopp"
Hardware	Mirabella's Hardware
Department Store	Uncle's Department Store
Butcher's	Piedmont Butcher's—Joe (Gallicano) the
	Butcher—Della-Badia's
Barber Shop's	Gabby's Barber Shop—Mike the Barber—Joe
	Marcelino's
Pizza Parlor's	Viccaro's Pizza Parlor—Johnnie's Kitchen
	Washington Ave Grill (then) Mario's
Chicken Market	Third Street Live Poultry Market
Liquor	Colombo Liquor's—Vitulli's Liquor
Supermarket	Caruso's Supermarket
Shoe Store	Cappelino's Shoe Store
Funeral Home	Cancro's Funeral Home

Car Repair	Joe Mauro (Antique Cars)—Zari's Gas Station—
Pool Hall	Union Ave Pool Hall
Iron Works	Charla Iron Works
Factory	Airquipt Factory
Construction Companies:	Bombace—Dandry—Calgi
Fish Market	Union Ave Fish Market
Social Clubs	North Italy Hall
Insurance	Mario DiMondo Insurance
Luncheonette	Tropical Casino
Doctor's	Dr. Newman (Dentist)—Dr.'s Marino & Brindisi
Traveling Trucks	Dominick Corbo the Iceman—Sal Pace Ice Man Pete Gambardella—Fruits & Vegetable's Sal Esposito with the Fruit's and Vegetable

On the other side of Webster Ave were more Stores:
Caruso's Supermarket—(2nd Store)
Nicolette's Pharmacy
Goodman's Fountain—Stationary & Candy Store
Casa Calabria Italian Society Hall
Glen Sport Shop
Ritacco's Gas Station

Washington & Webster & Saccone's

Zito's

Cancro

Marciano's

Popeye's store and "Popeye" as mentioned in chapter 5 was a very characteristic person. Small in stature and as mentioned had some sort of bone structure disease as he limped awkwardly. But everyone and I mean everyone loved Popeye. He was never mean to the kids and always had a smile. He was very friendly with the kids and as I mentioned earlier he loved baseball and loved talking about the Yankees of the 50's and early 60's. He loved Yogi Berra. His "Store" was located on the corner of Fifth St. & Union Ave. A small store with a "back room with a few friends always hanging out." He had a couple of glass cases with candy and packs of Tops baseball cards for sale. When you walked the street all you heard was "Hey Popeye" and *Yes*—men and woman walked in and out and everyone knew why but as a kid you just thought that's the way it was!!!!

Cannata's Candy Store located on the corner of Union Ave and Sixth St. was dingy, old, dusty and not very desirable for buying candy. I remember a long string going across the store with all the pictures of the Ballentine Girls of the Month winners. It was hanging there for years and out dated some 5 years! Just a head shot nothing vulgar. I believe Rossi's grandmother owned and operated the candy store and I imagine years before me it was probably a nice grocery store but as the grandmother got old the store got old. The way I remember it—it wasn't much of a store any more. Very dark and grungy with a few old glass cases with some penny candy. Most of the St. Joseph younger kids stopped in there a bought some candy during lunch or on there way home from school. *I didn't go in there too much, too dusty!* The grandmother always wore black and sat in front of the store all day and talked Italian to the neighbors. Rossi was a nice kid. Quite and didn't leave the corner too much as I remember him.

Cooney's Candy& Stationary Store—An I-con of an establishment. To this day all you hear about from the old timers is Cooney', Millie's & Saccone's. But Cooney's was something special in the "West." I remember the two overly large woman working behind the counter. Nice ladies and always pleasant to us kids. We would get everything at Cooney's candy, newspapers, envelopes small toys but I remember always running there to buy a whiffle ball. Cooney's name will forever be remembered to the people of the 50's and 60's.

Goose Generoso Candy Store—Located on the corner of Second St. and Lafayette Ave. Goose was another guy that loved baseball. In fact all of his kids especially Jimmy and Chico were terrific ball players of baseball and basketball. But Goose wasn't so much into selling much of any candy to kids. Us kids didn't go in Goose's too much because it had it's own cliental. But in the warm months Goose and the men hung out on the corner talking sports all day from what I remember as we always walked by in the neighborhood.

Millie's Grocery Store was located on Union Ave across the street from Viccaro's Pizza.—Millie is certainly one of the I-cons when it comes to growing up in the "West." Millie was just an amazing person on how she could cut cold-cut meats and handle customers. Because of the turn over rate of lunch meat that she sliced her cold-cuts always were the best tasting sandwiches anywhere! She worked alone the way I remember it and on Sunday morning she would have a store full of people after each church mass and it was amazing on how she sliced bagged and took care of customers. It was just astounding to watch how she had her black crayon and marked all the prices on the brown paper bag and wham! Add up all the items like she had a adding machine in her head....*Unbelievable how she did it!*

As I mentioned No One had a better tasting Bologna & Cheese sandwich with a fresh garden tomato on a kaiser roll with mustard or mayonnaise.

Millie had a full case of Italian cold-cuts. Another thing about Millie she could cut your cold-cuts so nice and thin which always gave it a better taste for whatever reason.

If I remember, Millie lived in the back of the grocery store because I remember that curtain that hung going into a kitchen where you can see her husband sitting all the time eating.

Millie had a few jars and bottles on the shelf's but Millie's was known for bread, milk, soda, fresh cold-cut meats and her making of sandwiches....*I miss Millie's!*

Immediato's Grocery Store located on the corner of Union Ave and Seventh St. (as I mention in chapter 3) was also as I remember it very old and the kind of place where you ran to get some milk, eggs or soda. Not too many people got there lunch meat there as everyone went to Millie's.

Sacco's Grocery Store located on the corner of Union Ave and Fourth St. was a grocery store of the 60's. You walk in and everything was built out of old wood. The shelves and the floor. There were a few items on the shelf like maybe macaroni and some jars of olives or beans. But most of the items were in bushels and barrels. All the fruit were in bushels like the peaches and pears. Other bushels would contain potato's, ears of corn or whatever was in season. There were bushels of nuts and seeds and like I mentioned in prior chapters Sacco had huge barrels of pigeon feed that was used for us local pigeon breeders.

Sacco had these old metal hanging scales all over the store so you can weigh the fruits and vegetables and pigeon feed.

There were two rooms to the store and you would walk from the front of the store to the back of the store and occasionally you would see a little mouse run around the barrel and us kids would run like hell but it didn't bother Sacco.

You would never buy cold-cut meats or a sandwich but if you needed cigarettes, bread, cold beer or soda you ran to Sacco's to get it.

Sacco was a good guy. He was kind of big and scruffy. But always nice to us kids. When we went in to purchase a dollar's worth of pigeon feed he would always make it a big bag and make it much more then the dollars worth. I'm not sure if he was married or had kids but I do know that Sacco was a pigeon lover himself as he also raced pigeon's from the top of the roof with his coop.

Paolucci's Grocery & Deli located on Fourth St. between Union Ave and Washington Ave was a very clean deli. Dom the owner was a fanatic for cleanness. No dust on the shelves, floor shinning. Everything on the shelf was stacked neatly, in order and all the labels facing out. Dom stocked everything, all kinds of canned goods. Stacks of Italian bread and the cold-cut case of meats were all in order meat after meat. As you walk in the deli the bell on the door would ring and the aroma of fresh bread would catch your nose. You immediately notice how clean the deli was. I always bought a turkey sandwich on a "club roll" with lots of mayonnaise, salt & pepper. To this day I never was able to duplicate that good tasting sandwich Dom would make me. Dom usually worked alone but eventually Danny Costa went to work for Dom as Dom would go home early and Danny would work till closing and clean the deli in the process.

Sunday's were very busy for Dom. The Sunday Newspaper was his big seller. The Daily News, The Daily Mirror, The Standard Star and The New York Times kept the floor filled with the thick newspapers.

People started to go for fresh cold-cut meats on Sundays as well as Dom started to have a following of steady customers after church mass as Millie's did....Dom had two great kids Rob and Emmylou.

Mirabella's Grocery Store located on the corner of Fourth St. and Washington Ave directly across the street from his two brothers and there store Mirabella's Hardware Store.

Mirabella's was a nice grocery store that to this day hasn't really changed much except the name. Nothing special about Mirabella's as people like the Mirabella brothers and switched off from one grocery store to another when it came to purchasing the usual items like eggs, bread, beer, soda and cigarettes. Mostly people from Washington Ave around third street to second street frequent Mirabella's the way I recall. I remember brothers Nick and Frank had the grocery store. I also remember Mirabella on a Sunday was usually the last to close by 12 noon and the first to re-open by 4pm. You remember stores closed for the afternoon on Sunday's back then—"Blue Law" If you needed something on a Sunday after 4pm you could always depend on Mirabella to be open....*Run to get that pack of cigarettes!*

Amori's Grocery Store was located on Sickles Ave between Fourth St and Madeline Ave. I didn't go there much and I think the owners name was Ed. If I happen to be playing as a kid on Sickles Ave with Timothy Hannigan or playing ball with Lenny Mecca like I said I never really went to Amori's store. What I remember was this small store that you had to step down to go into. The store served it's purpose for all the "West Ender's" from Madeline or Sickles Ave's.

Gurrieri's Grocery Store was located on the corner of Union Ave and Fourth St. "Mousey Gurrieri"—a great guy and a couple of years younger then me was a nice kid. Always smiling and a pretty good baseball player. "Mouse" as we called him lived in the corner building and I believe it was his Grandmother who operated the grocery store. It later became a pretty good luncheonette serving very good burgers. The grocery store was no different from all the other stores and served its' purpose as the others.

Rocco Bellontoni's Grocery Store was located on Second St opposite Grove Ave near the Airquipt Factory. Rocco and his family ran the business. Another store I didn't go in much since it was a few blocks from me. But Rocco as I remember became a big name in the "West" and then around New Rochelle and then Westchester County as he had some pretty good political ties as I remember and very much of a community activist.

Zito's Pharmacy was like our family doctor. It was located on the corner of Union Ave and Fourth St. If you had a cold or weren't feeling well you went to see Mr. Zito who would always tell you what to take for your aliment or pain.

We would take our little medication container that was prescribed by the family doctor and watch him type out a label on the old typewriter and take it to the back of the pharmacy for refilling as we would go back in a few hours. Behind him on the counter he would have all the medication containers all lined up ready for pick up.

He had a very nice pharmacy with glass cases on both sides filled with shampoo, soap perfume and other items. He also had some very inexpensive gifts for purchase. I remember when I would save all my pennies and nickels from my Halloween collection "Trick & Treat Bag." I would then go to Zito's pharmacy and Christmas shop for presents. I was about 8 or 9 years old. I remember one present I purchased was shampoo mixed with beer for my sister. *She loved it!* My mom and dad I would always get some sort of powder for mom and soap on a rope for dad.

Zito's also had all those Norman Rockwell pictures on the walls from the old Saturday Evening Post Magazine. Mr. Zito also had those antique medical instruments on display.

As I said if you had an ailment you went to see Mr. Zito first. Most of the time he would take care of you unless it was very serious then it was to the family doctor who of course would make a home visit.

Joe's Shoe Repair on Union Ave was your typical shoe repair store. In fact to this day if you do find an old shoe repair store they sure haven't changed much. Just a small shop with all those wheels & brushes spinning with shoes all over the place that were waiting to be picked up or haven't been picked up in years. You would also find on the shelves all the slates of leather soles and heels. That was the best part of Joe's he would give us leather heels so we can have some huge Hop-Scotch games. *"Yes" us boys played also just for fun with the girls!* We would walk in as kids and say "Hey Joe can I have a heel for Hop-Scotch" and he would throw us one as he was brushing a shoe on the big wheel.

Joe took good care of our shoes. Times were tough, you didn't go buy shoes to often. So if you had a hole in the sole or needed heels we would bring them to Joe and he would put the soles, heels, taps on them. If you needed supplies like shoe polish or shoe strings you went to Joe's Shoe Repair. A great local community guy who loved us kids!

Galatti's Bakery was also located on Fourth St. directly behind Paolucci's Deli. You had to walk down the alleyway and driveway to get to the bakery. I remember "Red Galati" ran the bakery. Known for their fresh homemade baked bread it always had a different taste then West Side bakery or Marciano's bread. But very good and as I mentioned with Dom's turkey sandwich on a "Club Roll" that he made for me the "Club Roll" came from Galatti's. They also made some delicious Sunday morning buns.

The business and warehouse wasn't as big as West Side bakery. But they had a lucrative business that did very well. A few trucks for delivery but "Red" and family made a very good go at it for many years.

West Side Bakery was located on Third St. between Union Ave and Washington Ave. A huge red brick building that took up most of the block. What I remember most about West Side Bakery is when they baked their bread and the rolls and they were done around 8:30pm in the evening in the summer time you could smell that wonderful aroma of fresh warm bread in the air for block after block in the neighborhood. From Third St. to Ninth St. So you can imagine where I lived on Fifth St. mmmm it smelled so good!

Every night in the summer about that time 9-9:15pm I would go to West Side Bakery and enter the side green door and bag my own dozen rolls. I would then run back home as fast as I can so to keep the warmth of the freshly new baked rolls nice and hot!

When I got home my mother or sister would then slice open that Kaiser roll and the steam would come floating out and the butter would just melt when spreading it on it. *Delicious*—I was like a little hero running home as fast as I can so the family could have nice hot rolls as a snack after our carvel ice cream bar.

I liked going to the West Side Bakery. There were times the bread rolls were a little late for sale and I would wait. I used to love to walk around and was marveled to look above at the rolling tracks hanging from the ceiling and how the bread would go from one section at a time from the baker to the oven to the end of the assembly line to where they where bagged and ready for the truck and delivery. I would walk around to see all the different breads being made. *I guess it was just a fascinating thing as a kid watching the process.* For whatever reason the bakery didn't like people to come in during the winter at night to purchase bread. I really never found out the reason nor did I ever try to find out. It was just an acceptable thing you didn't go in the winter to West Side Bakery....Who owned West Side Bakery anyway? Good question! I never knew, do you?

Marciano's Bakery located on Union Ave between First St. and Second St. in what was called the "Marciano Flat" because it was the ground floor of a 4-5 story apartment building.

What I remember that the bakery was small and old and didn't look like what you would called a bakery. They baked and sold bread, buns and very good Italian pastries. But what I remember that in the late 60's was my dad would take our Thanksgiving Turkey there to be cooked. He would have to drop it off very early about 5am and then pick it up by 1pm. That really helped as my mom would be able to use the oven for the lasagna and other food items for the Thanksgiving Feast.

If I remember they had a small store front with a few glass cases and I remember walking down the alleyway to where the ovens where. They weren't big on retail I think most of their sales were store deliveries. But for years Marciano's was a household name in the neighborhood and around New Rochelle.

"The Cake Shopp" Bakery located on Union Ave. between Second St. and Third St. was a very nice bakery but to be honest I don't remember to much about it. As a kid I didn't do much except for picking up a cake. Usually my mom or sister took care of that chore. I just remember a few glass cases with the usual Italian pastries that I didn't eat much of as a kid because I enjoyed "Yankee Doodle" cupcakes or the "Hostess" cupcake with the white little scribbled lines across it. So as a kid cannoli's or other pastries didn't interest me until of course I got a little older.

Mirabella's Hardware Store was located on the corner of Washington Ave & Fourth St directly across the street from Mirabella's grocery store. Brothers Charlie and Mike operated the store. The hardware store was our direct link for any tools, paint, nails, screws or home goods such as cleaning supplies etc. Mirabella's wasn't Lowe's or Home Depot or a Ace Hardware, they were not in existence yet. You need supplies Mirabella's was the hardware store you can depend on. In the late 60's, maybe even

1970 if I remember Tony Montaleone the guy who kept his cars nice and shiny on Fifth St ended up buying the store and kept it up for good while. I'm not sure when he sold it but by then I was out of High School and out of the neighborhood.

Uncle's Department Store located on Union Ave between Fourth St. and Third St....All I really remember was Judy Morgan working the store as a sales clerk. I don't know if she and the family owned it or if she just worked there. But it was a nice one floor store that served the community for clothing. I use to get my winter gloves there along with some items that mom purchased like socks, underwear, T-shirts and a shirt here and there. I also remember as a kid that Judy Morgan was well known in the neighborhood and that she was good friends with a gentleman by the name as we called him "Joe Biff."

Piedmont's Butcher Shop located on the corner of Fourth St. and St. Johns Pl. was owned and operated if I remember by Joe Piedmont. They served mostly the other end of the "West" from where I lived from Fifth St., mainly the Sickles, Madeline Ave side of the "West." I remember a friend of mind from school Mario Carpanzano use to go in at night to clean the wood butcher blocks and the floor. He would let me use the telephone to call girls and we would be on the phone for 2-3 hours calling up everyone we knew. I couldn't call from home since we only had one telephone on the kitchen wall and mom wasn't going to allow me to use up what she called "Units" all night yakking to girls. But what I was told Piedmont's had very good fresh meats and was one of the better butcher shops.

Joe (Gallicano) the Butcher located on Washington Ave between Fifth St. and Fourth St. The best thing I remember about Joe's that as kids we would go into Joe's after playing baseball at Columbus school and Joe would throw us a raw frankfurter with no bun of course. He also made a very good sausage and pepper wedge. He would let us sit in the back and eat it or we would sit on the front steps and Joe would give us free soda with it. Other then that I don't remember more about "Joe the Butcher" except that Joe loved us kids and loved throwing us a raw Hot Dog!...

Was his meat in the case good? I guess it was, the Hot dogs were even if they were raw!....Thanks Joe for the Dogs!

Della-Badia's Butcher shop was located on the corner of Washington Ave and Fourth St. The little I remember that butcher shop was there before "Joe the Butcher" opened up—up the street. There is a bank there now for years. That's all I remember about Della-Badia's Butcher Shop. Maybe some of you old timers might remember the shop from the 50's

Barber Shop's in the "West'....(Three) I Remember....

The Barber Shop's I remember in the "West"—There was Gabi's on Fourth St next to Piedmont's Butcher Shop, then there was Mike the Barber on Fourth St. next to Paolucci's Deli and Galati's Bakery and then their was Joe Marcelino's Barber shop on Union Ave next to Uncle's Department Store.

I used to go to Mike the Barber. I used too get a kick of walking up the stairs and sitting in the chair high up as the cars and people walked by. Joe Marcelino's was a little too fancy for me as I remember it. My brother used to go to that Barber shop. My father used to go to Gabe's because the son was married to his niece or my cousin however you look at it.

I remember the late 60's when long hair was in. The old timers were still going to the barber shop but kids to teens weren't going as often and there was all kind of deals and gimmicks to get people in the barber shops. They started to call it "Hair Styling's cut for long hair. Open up the barber shop to woman. *Anything to stay open.* Then the prices started to go up and then finally they started to close.

I believe Joe Marcelino moved his shop to downtown New Rochelle on Division St.

Pizza Parlors....

Viccaro's Pizza Parlor is very well described in Chapter (5). All about it's location on Union Ave between Fifth St and Sixth St. and how it is operated by the Viccaro family from the grandfather down. I wrote about the garden of fresh grown tomato's and vegetables. I wrote about the restaurant and the bar and it's service operation. The food was simply the best ever. The pizza, the macaroni and it's hero's were something you very rarely endure and taste today at restaurants. I just wish I was a little older to really enjoy a sit down dinner as opposed to some kid gobbling down pizza or a sandwich!

I also wrote about Johnnie's Kitchen on the corner of St. John's Place and Fourth St. in the previous chapter and how Johnnie's left the "West" and open Giovanni's Restaurant on Main St.

I remember walking up the stairs into the restaurant to order a slice of pizza and sitting in the back of the restaurant with a couple of small windows.

Washington Grill then it became "Mario's." A nice size restaurant that had a nice bar on one side and a restaurant on the other side. I remember the stir it caused in the neighborhood when they hired Go-Go Dancers and they used to dance on a table. Kids would sneak by the window in the summer and peak to see the girls dancing. The food was good and in fact from what I remember the pizza was pretty good. A lot of the "West End" resident's had family parties in the restaurants for the kids for communions, birthday's etc.

Third Street Live Poultry Chicken Market was located on Third St just off Union Ave behind the Calgi Construction Office. Everyone has a memory about the chicken market. I don't care how old you were you remember some experience about the market. Everyone went to the chicken market and was amazed in what they saw. I remember walking into a big room and of course the poultry were just running loose. You picked out your chicken and then they brought it out to the side room and placed it in the machine with this churning type of wheel and the next thing I remember was a lot of noise and feathers flying all over the place and you were then walking home with your fresh killed chicken.

Colombo Liquors was located on Union Ave between First St & Second St. The Colombo's the way I remember it lived on Madeline Ave and besides having the Liquor Store they too had a pigeon coop and was part of the racing pigeon circuit as I wrote about in chapter 5.

Vitulli Liquors was located on Fourth St. across the street from Cancro's Funeral Home. The one story I remember about Vitulli's was some years later I think it was the bank on the corner had got robbed and Mr. Vitulli came out and shot his handgun at the would be thief's. I Don't remember if he hit them or not or they were eventually caught but I believe he was given an award and a big write up in the newspaper.

Caruso's Supermarket located on the corner of Union Ave and Second Street. The supermarket was owned and operated by the Caruso family. Everyone in the family was involved in some capacity.

Besides being known as the only real supermarket in the "West" it was also well known for July 4th celebration and its contents.

The biggest fire work display right there on the corner in the middle of the street was a show in it's self to watch!

Cappelino's Shoe Store was located on Union Ave directly across the street from Uncle's Department store between Fourth St. and Third Street. The store had a store front but the store itself was small. The entrance to the house for the family was on the side since the front door was used for the shoe store. It was located in part and in front of the Cappelino House where my friend Tommy Cappelino lived.

Tommy and I went to Columbus School together. We played on the same Little League Team and Boys Club Team together as 12 year olds.

You had to walk or step down into the store and just like any other shoe store had shelves of shoes with a few shoes on display in the small window. Tommy's grandfather worked the shoe store and was always very patient and helpful.

I remember buying everyday leather black (work shoe) type of boot. Great for everyday winter wear. I also purchased my dress shoes at Cappelino's. But that was before I was able to go to Main St and buy my shoes either at Hardy's, Thom Mcan or National Shoe Stores.

Cancro's Funeral Home located now on Fourth St. between Washington Ave and St. John's Place. As a kid it was located down the block on Fourth St between Union Ave and Washington Ave until they built the new building and I'm guessing in the early 60's.

Everyone and everybody from the "West" who passed was waked at Cancro's.

Cancro's is a family business since about 1920 and now passed down at least three generations.

Cancro's always did the right thing for the neighborhood and the residents of "West" New Rochelle. Always very respectful and accommodating for the family's needs.

Cancro's always made it easy for the family in their sorrow times when making the arrangements.

Back in the 60's a wake lasted 3 days and 3 nights. Why because most of one's family all lived in the area or the "West." Not to mention the whole neighborhood came out for the wake and funeral. It just was the right thing to do for respect for the people from the "West End."

Everyone knew each other, everyone went to school together, everyone played sports together or just hung in the streets as kids together and just about everyone had their uncle's, aunts and grandparents in the neighborhood. So when it came to attending and show your respects it was well attended for 3 days and nights.

In time of need and sorrow the people of the "West" leaned on each other for comfort and peace for family and friends and Cancro's Funeral Home saw to it that it all was done in proper moments.

Car Repair....One thing I always found out about the 60's the vehicles were all American made cars. No computers, simple carburetor and mostly everyone worked on their own cars mechanically. But if there had to be work on a car a lot of people did work for someone from their garage, ala John Claps did as I mentioned in chapter 5.

But in the neighborhood their was Zari's garage on the corner of Washington Ave and Fourth St. The thing I'll always remember about Zari was that they were a big fan of the "Studebaker" car.

Joe Mauro's was located on Eight Street. Mr. Mauro was almost like a private type of car repair. You just didn't drive your car in their garage. Joe had to know you and he was very selective on what vehicles he worked on or repaired.

I do remember Mr. Mauro had some very nice antique vehicles and I will always remember that he had Gas Pumps on his front lawn!

Union Ave Pool Hall was located on Union Ave between Fifth St. and Fourth Street. Anyone from the 50's and 60's knew it all started from the Pool Hall. A social gathering of politics, everyday money matters and a lot of Italian language being heard. Yes they had pool tables and card tables but it was mostly a gathering of men talking about the old country in Italy, talking about sports and talking about the "number" of the day.

Although I never set foot in the Pool Hall us kids always when walking by marveled at it's desirable condition of always being known as the "Meeting" place. Us kids would try to look down the stairs into the darkness of the opening to see exactly what it was all about.

My Aunt Rita (we call her Aunt Leggett—my father's sister) with my grandfather along with her sons Juniee Boy, Alley Boy and Sammy (two daughters Lulu and Mary Doll were out of the house by then—Mary Doll married Phil Mercurio and Lulu married Andrew Perino.) lived above the Pool Hall. When I went with my father to visit my cousins I would sit outside on the front stoop and watch as men came and went in and out of the Pool Hall. As I mentioned Italian language, broken English would be loud and boisterous as everyone had a cigarette or cigar in their mouth. You couldn't talk unless you had either one dangling.

Their were the regulars who frequent the Pool Hall. Joe Biff, Jimmy the Blade, Popeye, Grippo and many others.

A social meeting place of the minds and as I said "Numbers."

Charla Iron Works as I remember were in (3) different locations of Iron Work Factories. All family members but the one I remember was Chick Charla. Now there was the Iron Works on the corner of Union Ave and Sixth Street and then there was the Iron Works on the corner of Fourth St. and St. Johns Pl. across from the old Johnnies Kitchen. The third Iron Works was down on Beechwood Ave past Bellontoni grocery.

Airquipt Factory located on the south side section of the whole block on Jones St. from Second St. to the to Webster Ave. The factory employed a lot of the resident's in the "West End" including Mauro's father. They made a lot of different parts for airplanes and for airports from what I remember. A lot of Government work which meant inspectors all the time according to Mauro.

Construction companies in the "West" also was a big part of hiring men from the "West"—I know one for sure was Danny Costa's dad "Coach" who drove a big dump truck for Bombace Construction. Other companies in the "West" were Dandry and Calgi Construction Companies. Calgi's office were located on the corner of Union Ave and Third Street. The Dandry family were located behind Feeney Park in the Green Place section of the "West" (one of the most beautiful and best kept secret area's in New Rochelle along with Edgewood Park Street.)

Union Ave Fish Market on Union Ave between Third Street and Second Street. A typical looking fish store from the 50's/60's. Fresh fish on ice in these big iron draws. All kind of fish with big mouths and big eyes looking up at you and man did it smell when you entered. But always crowded with ladies all dressed in black picking up, feeling, touching and handling all the fish. "How-much-a pound"—"Isita fesh" not to make fun of the broken Italian language but pretty intimidating when you are a kid getting pushed around by all these ladies with long black dresses, hair in a bun throwing fish around.

But the best I remember my mother loved to fry up eels. So she sent me to get the eels. One minute the eel is swimming around in the pool looking like a snake and then the next minute the butcher is chopping it up in pieces about a inch and a half long. The dam eel while getting cut up you can see all the parts are still moving around the table—it's still alive while being sliced up! I used to tell the butcher make sure that eel is dead before you wrap it and give it to me. Of course the butcher would make a motion in my face every time with the eel in the bag saying something like "Watcha out the eel-a gonna bite-ah youuu." with a nice big hardy laugh. With that I ran home to get that eel out of my hands to my mother.

North Italy Hall—The meeting place and social gathering of the "West"—In the 40's-50's a lot of the Italian couples had there wedding reception there with some of the finest Italian sandwiches you can taste and lots of homemade wine. Everyone would bring a dish or bake cookies for the wedding reception.

I remember going there with my father to hear Mayor (Elect) Frank Garito give his speech to the "West" residents thanking everyone for their support.

Mario DiMondo Insurance handled all the Italian families legal paper work. Helped everyone that needed guidance. Sold all kinds of insurance and helped in getting your license plates without going to White Plains as we all know it was not an easy task in those days at the motor vehicle office.

The DiMondo family were nice people that everyone looked up to from what I remember.

The Tropical Casino Restaurant & Bar was located on Union Ave next to Cappelino's Shoe Store. It was primarily African-Americans that patronized the Restaurant and Bar. You look in the Restaurant and you would see a long Bar with booth like tables and seats filling out the rest of the restaurant. It was always kept nice and I remember painted on the store front window were palm trees. You could always hear the juke box but it never bothered the neighborhood as it was just part of the "West" community.

Dr. Newman the Dentist of the "West" located on Washington Ave and Dr.'s Marino and Brindisi the Medical Doctor's from Webster Ave. What can you say about these fine Doctor's as they served the community with distinguished respect for all the families, who needed help with their expertise. It wasn't about money. It was about serving the "West" for the love of the community.

The Ice Man and the Fruit & Vegetable man coming down your street selling their product. The Ice man with his big huge ice cold clear block of ice. There was Dominick Corbo and their was Sal Pace. They had these old trucks with the ice and as kids in the hot summer we would run up to the truck and ask the Ice man for a piece of ice and they would cut off a big chunk and we would sit on the curb sucking on the big chunk of ice flipping it from one hand to the other because it was cold. With the hot summer days it didn't take long for the ice to melt and as it was dripping we would also rub it in our hair and face and along our arms.... *What great simple fun!*

We would watch the Ice man with his big huge iron claw grab the big block of ice and deliver it to the house or stores.

Then there was the coal man in there coal trucks delivering all the coal to the houses and to the back of Columbus School as we would watch the coal man slide the coal down the chute through the big iron door at Columbus School

The best were Pete Camardella and Sal Esposito with there Fruit & Vegetable trucks. First for the longest time it was Pete driving around the "West" with his loud voice yelling Fruits & Vegetable's in Italian and broken English. Then when Pete retired Sal came along. Both men were great to the kids. Throwing us long string beans, carrots, a peach or a banana. I remember Sal had this old red truck like a school bus and then one day he had this brand new powder blue truck with this beautiful painted scroll and his name on the side in white lettering. He said it cost him and lot of Fruits and Vegetables to have his name painted on the side. Sal lived on Madeline Ave overlooking Feeney Park. He had a tremendous voice bellowing out among the neighorboorhood and when he yelled his script of what he was selling he would always finish up with "and Wallenmelonnnn"...

I Love Those Men....

Chapter (7)

"Columbus School"

Columbus Elementary Grammar School, the old Columbus School. Located on Washington Ave between 5th Street and 7th Street. (You would think as I mention prior that Columbus School would have been named Washington School instead of Columbus since it was located on Washington Ave. Instead Washington School was located up on the beginning of Union Ave....*Anyway,* A beautiful brick solid mosaic school built like all the ole schools back in the early 20's-30's. You go to the Bronx and you see a lot of the similarities of Columbus School still on the corners of the Bronx. Same style. White Brick with the huge windows. Big black iron fire escapes.

Columbus School from I heard was the first High School in New Rochelle. Not sure if that was true. But anyway, a huge building some five stories high.

On the Washington Ave side was the statue of Columbus. The main entrance was on Washington with a brick wall that ran along Washington Ave with a black wrought iron fence attached on top along the wall. The main entrance was not used anymore. Us kids would enter the school from behind the building. I guess the main entrance was used years ago. But we entered through the back entrance while the teachers and administration entered from Washington Ave opposite 6th Street.

I loved that school with its hard wooded floors, cement hallway floors. Layers of paint on the walls. Of course the bathrooms were huge and roomy! I loved the windows with the huge poles to reach up to open and close with the big brown shades.

Columbus School

IL-COLUMBUS SCHOOL-1957-58

My 1ˢᵗ Grade Class @ Columbus School
(My Bird Picture—Left of the Door)
Bottom Row—"Middle"

Can you find me sitting in the Class?

Kids in Class

Albert Ferretti
Tina Passarelli
Richard Zippilli
Diane Gregory
Gary Summo
Dominick Amorsano
Susan Samela
Carmine Gentile
Tim Hannigan
Camille Immediato
Barbara Strazza

John Caruso
Debbie Burrioni
Vincent Beard
John Hollis
Gloria Starpoli
John Creaco
Frank Caruso
Glenn Decker

First Grade

As I remember the old Columbus School was built basically within two separate buildings. One building was built along and facing Washington Ave while the other section although connected basically faced 7th street. You can see what I mean by the picture on the next page.

The building facing 7th St. had of course the huge black top and dirt/grass baseball/playgrounds that ran along Washington Ave up to 7th St.

The second building contained as I remember it the beautiful huge auditorium with it's hanging chandelier lights. It had the old wide wooden seats. As I mentioned prior you can still find those seats in some of the Bronx schools as I did at Lehman High School on Tremont Ave in the Bronx. Those seats at Columbus and at Lehman may be made out of that hard brown wood but they were a little wider then these new seats and they can last forever and yes comfortable too! The auditorium had a huge balcony and huge stage.

The windows as seen from 7th St. and from the playground were tremendous, some three stories high. Beautiful concave tops that were decorated with it's gorgeous drapes, maroon in color as I remember it. Under the auditorium were the gymnasiums. One for the Boys (which was a little larger) and another gym to the other side for the girls. The boys gym was a typical gym with it's climbing ropes and other apparatus. There was an entrance from the gym that lead out to the playground.

In the rear of Columbus School behind the building that faced 7th St. were the old black fire escapes. Us kids got a big kick out of the fire drills and walking down the fire escapes. Don't ask me why but being up 4 or 5 stories and in the open air with just a wrought iron between us and the air made it feel like some sort of exciting adventure like riding on a "playland" ride.

If you were lucky enough to be given the chore or job to clean the blackboard erases you were able to go out onto the fire escape and clean them. It wasn't the thrill of cleaning the erases by banging them together it was again, the thrill of standing out on the fire escape over looking the backyards of the houses from St. John's Pl. and Madeline Ave.

To the left of the fire escape were the two huge smoke stacks that were connected to the old coal bin area. Again us kids got a thrill as we watched when the coal trucks would come and load the coal into the big black iron clad gate with the coal shooting down the belt. Behind the building was a small blacktop playground that went between the building and the backyards.

There were also steps that lead behind the corner of both buildings to a small alleyway that lead to the huge playground. Now if you were in grades K thru 3 you would have to report or play in the small playground before the school bell rang for line up for class. But grades 4-6 had the opportunity and were able to go down the stairs and play in the big playground while waiting for the school bell. I know, no big deal but back then you couldn't wait to get into the 4th grade so you can walk down the steps to the big playground.

Part of getting older I guess and getting bigger who knows why the thrill of walking down those steps to the bigger playground!... lol

It is of my opinion that knocking down the old Columbus School was a mistake. I know it was cheaper to build a new school then to upgrade the old school with plumbing and electrical etc. But it seems to me that all those old schools as I mentioned from the Bronx, Brooklyn, Queens seem to be still very useful and I feel Columbus Elementary School could have been saved and upgraded.

The new Columbus School just does not have the character and charm the old Columbus School had.

Inside the old school were the wide stair steps with the big hand railings. High ceilings etc.

As I mentioned prior I was told that Columbus School was once a High School so there was a section of the building that was closed to the students and staff and not in use of classrooms. I remember that the building was not secure and you could sneak into the other side. There were times when myself, Gloria Starpolli and a couple of other classmates would sneak into the building. We were on the School Safety Patrol as monitors. Safety Patrol Officers had these beautiful badges shaped like police badges. If you were a regular guard your badge was all silver. If you were a Sergeant it had a green inner color on the New York State Symbol. If you were a lieutenant the inner color was red and of course if you were the Captain it was colored with a blue lining around the NYS symbol.

We would report to our posts before classes started. When school would end and also just before the students reported back from lunch break. You had to be in at least the 4th grade to be a safety patrol officer. The 4th graders usually manned the halls and stair ways. Your job was to keep the kids walking on one side of the hall and watching the stairs. Their was usually a Sergeant and a Lieutenant assigned to a floor and the Captain would patrol all the floors.

So anyway back to the section of the school that was not being used any longer. We would sneak into the building. It was creepy! Water puddles, creaky floors, paint coming off the walls and very dark. Of course as kids you thought the worst of some sort of spooky feeling that made it very eerie walking around. Nothing to look at but old desks and dusty old furniture. But it made it a fun thing to do at the time!

Now I have to talk about the Columbus School playground. I am on record from years ago by saying the biggest and I mean the biggest mistake the New Rochelle School Board or the City Council Elected Officials or both agencies made was the destroying of the playground and taking it away from the "West End" neighborhood to make way for the new construction of Columbus Elementary School.

Every kid that grew up from the 50's-60's and right up till they built the new school has vivid memories of playing on that playground. Starting with the afternoon school programs and signing out for basketballs, softballs, baseball bats, kickball's and whatever other recreation from Nello Amori.

Nello worked for the New Rochelle Recreation Department and was assigned to the playground and it seems like he was there forever! On Saturday in the summer we would play horseshoes. The horseshoe pits were set up by alleyway that led up to the upper or building playground. On those hot summer days they had the water sprinkler going for us kids. Man did that feel good running through the water. As I mentioned before when you walked in from the Washington Ave side that part of the playground was blacked topped with painted out softball/kickball lines with bases. Along the school you would play stickball or hand ball against the wall. They had painted hopscotch lines and had a couple of volleyball nets up with these home made poles cemented in these tin cans to hold up the net that eventually would sag at some point. The basketball nets were also up against the school.

On summer nights the playground was jammed with kids from all over the neighborhood. Softball, hardball games going on. People from all over the neighborhood watching the games. You can hear the clanging of the horseshoes. As I said, vivid memories for anyone growing up in that era!

We hated Wednesday nights because they would use the playground as a parking lot for the Wednesday night bingo at the Boy's Club.

The playground was out of use for that evening. So it was to the streets to play kickball, stickball or a game like "Hide & Go Seek" or better yet sitting on Mauro's garage roof gazing at the summer stars after a nice Good Humor Ice Cream from Pete! We liked sitting on Mauro's garage because we can jump from 2-3 different garage roofs!

There was all kinds of baseball/softball games going on. There were the adult fast pitch league. There was the youth hardball leagues. Their was the 12 and under old kids playing softball on the blacktop and then there were the girls softball played as well on the black top. The fast pitch league was great to watch. I was about 10 when I would see Bill Marino with one arm pitch with his great wind up. Then there was Billy Telesco (I think the name of the team was called "AAA Trucking" if my memory serves me right.) Billy was a big strong lefty and everyone would come to watch him hit while they waited to see if he was going to knock one out into Mr. Esposito's yard which seemed like a mile away when you're a kid.

When I was about 12-13 years old I played in the hard ball league. Tommy Cappolino and myself jumped back and forth from the Boy's Club league to Little League. The Boys Club league was coached by Jim Generoso dad. He was the City Clerk or Court Clerk at the time, I forget which one he worked at for the City of New Rochelle. Anyway Jimmy who is now the Court Clerk in New Rochelle was on the team as well as his cousin Chico. We had a great team with guys like Chico, Dale Long, Walter Vale, Larry Fredricks and Tommy. I still have a signed ball from a All-Star Game from July 15th, 1963 *WoW 50+ Years ago*

All–Star Game Ball 1963

Signed by
Chico Generoso & Larry Fredrick's

Signed by Sal Generoso

Signed by Umpire DiPippo

The best part of Columbus School playground was the pick up hardball baseball games we would have. On Saturday afternoon when they would lock the gate or on Sunday afternoon (after our Sunday macaroni and if we didn't go visiting to see some family) we would climb over the gate and have some big time choose up games from kids from all over the neighborhood. The Burigo brothers would be there. Lenny Mecca might come by, Chico was there and so on.

We also had some good times and softball games by playing Home Run Derby—A spin off from the old T.V. Home Run Derby show we used to see on the TV with the "Mick—Willie—Rocky Colivito" and others. We would see how many we can hit over the fence onto 7th Street. Another huge game was a 3 man game of stickball. A Pitcher and 2 outfielders. We would draw the box on the wall for the strike zone. We then went to Cooney's for a new pink Spaulding. At times if nothing else a good ole tennis ball would do.

Now to top off a great Hot Summer Saturday afternoon after a big game we would go across the street to Saccone's for our Lemon Ice that cost 10 cents and if we had a few more pennies we were able to buy a couple of rod pretzels to dunk into Saccone's home made lemon ice. Anyone from the "West" knows what I am talking about! Just "THE BEST" lemon ice anywhere at the time. We would watch Nunzi with his shovel and he had a knack the way he would scoop the lemon ice out of the bucket and fill the little white paper cup.

In the early days of Saccone's facing the Washington Ave side. The window from the store was this little pushed up window that had a silver tin covering....Shack type opening at the time. So in closing about the Columbus School playground, like I said a huge mistake shrinking it down the size when the new Columbus School was built. Real bad move.... Like the song from Madonna... *"There used to be a Playground there"* - .... *sad ending....*

CHAPTER (8)

"Saint Joseph Church & School"

When you think of Saint Joseph Church you think of one thing or one person. Father Aldo Carniato and of course the image of the Father walking along Washington Ave in his black robe walking his dog.

The grounds and the buildings which include the church, rectory, convent and school are just so much part of the "West" as there is when it comes to history and memories that make up a big part of each and every catholic that lived in the "West End" of New Rochelle. In the sixties the nuns were so inspirational and monumental in the studies of the residents of the "West." If you went to St. Joseph School you lived by the rule of the nuns. If you didn't go to the school you lived by the rule of the nuns in relig or at Sunday mass. They were so much a part of the "West" as all of us Italians or Catholics were as we lived our lives while growing up in that area and era.

The nuns taught you obedience, character and respect. Yes at times they screamed at you, pulled your ear or whacked you with their white prayer rope! But the nuns demanded obedience and most of the times they were sensitive and thoughtful to your faith.

The convent was always so solemn, secured and mysterious. When you walked by you always looked at the building (that was located basically on the corner of 5th Street & Union Ave.) You couldn't help but to look up at the black wooden building and up at the windows and as a young kid as you wondered what was going on inside. It seemed that the nuns didn't walk around the neighborhood too much or as I remember it didn't seem like that to me. Although there were many times you would see the nuns walking around the grounds of the school and behind the church paired off praying.

St. Joseph Church

I didn't attend St. Joseph School as a student only to Wednesday afternoon religious and instruction so I really don't remember any of the names of the nuns. When I was in my 20's I did have a part time job at the school as a Gym Instructor a couple of days a week. I would take each class for an hour and escort them to the Boy's Club for some exercise and recreation with Fran Mucci. If I remember the principal's name at the time was Sister Grace or Sister Mary Grace?

As we all know by now St. Joseph School has been shut down to learning studies. It was a learning center for K thru 8th grade. My thought at the time of the closing some years ago was why not down grade first before closing of the whole school. My thoughts run the school from K thru 5th or 6th grade. But it was of course up to the Catholic Archdiocese of New York as there was a wave of closing Catholic Schools throughout the area.

St. Joseph School served a very instrumental part of the "West" with the teaching from the nuns to civilian staff. It was great for the neighborhood with its blue & white uniforms worn by the students. The tuition was very affordable for the "West End" families as it served the faith of the Catholic Religion in a manor of setting a situational foundation of love & prayer for the Lord for the present and latter years in life on personal and family lifestyle.

The School was old, no doubt about it. Repairs were costly, the neighborhood, the church members, the Holy Name Society of the church all tried to keep it going. But as time went on the breakdown and cost along with a declining admission of students the school could not survive the everyday expenditure. Ultimately ending up with no choice but for the Archdiocese to close the school down.

I had my share of memories of St. Joseph School as well as the Church. Like I mentioned I didn't attend the school except for Wednesday afternoon Religious and Instruction. Every Wednesday afternoon the Columbus School Catholic students would walk across the street and attend class at St. Joseph School. The students and kids of St. Joe's loved it, they got out of school an hour and a half earlier.

We learned what we learned regarding the catholic religion as well as preparing us for our First Holy Communion and then blessed with our Sacrament of Confirmation. Most of us were Baptized as babies except those that came over from Italy.

I never experienced marriage but I can tell you that many of the "West Enders" that did, all received their Sacrament of Marriage at St. Joseph including my sister Diane on that faithful stormy rainy day in May in 1965. I have some fond memories of coaching sports with St. Joseph Students. Kids at the time like Peter Veltri, Joe Nicole, Frank Daniele, Louis Vitulli, Joe Colangelo etc....I coached Basketball and Baseball. They used to love to go to the old Wedge Inn on Boston post Road in the Bronx after practice.

If you attended Columbus School as a student you weren't allowed to serve as an alter boy for the church. A horrible rule that a lot of us Columbus kids regretted and felt bad about. But there was one kid that was able to serve as an alter boy from Columbus School. How it happened to this day I don't know how. But he was accepted and was serving mass on Sunday's. His name was Richard and we will leave it at that!!!....Girls were not yet allowed to serve at that time. Another terrible rule that was eventually changed.

My good friend Mauro Viccaro was an alterboy and man I have a lot of good memories with Mauro. Mauro would go on a Saturday afternoon to set up and prepare for church and mass. At that time in the 60's there was no Saturday Masses. There was no one in the church since confession was over. Mauro would take me in the back and of course curious young adolescent kids doing some things that were probably a little sac-religious at the time. Nothing vicious or of any criminal activity or destroying any property. No stealing or anything like that just some mischievous doings. Like we would look in the closest and eat some of the host or the sacrament bread that is used for mass. We at times well maybe me would put on some of the priest clothing like one of the stoles that I would drape around my neck or put on the Robe/Chasubles. Mauro who was at the alter preparing for the next day would walk back into the room and freak out screaming "take that off"—"if Father Carniato walks in he will kill us."—Got to tell you Mauro and I did taste a little of the wine that is also used for the Host of Sacrament of Bread. I know Mauro will not admit to it but believe me he did lol.

There was a time a young priest was assigned and joined St. Joseph. He was very nice but don't ask me his name I have no idea. But after confession he would come out to the front of the church on the steps and talk to anyone coming out of the church. So this one afternoon myself along with Mauro and a couple of other people were out in front of the church. Mauro for some reason thought this priest could somehow know things about people with some sort of inner power. So I thought I play a trick on Mauro, confidently while Mauro was talking to someone I said to the priest "Ask Mauro about a certain girl he likes in the neighborhood." Well when the priest said "How is it going boys"? And Mauro I sense you like a girl named Gail"? Mauro almost shit in front of the Priest.

Sis-Holy Comm

DN-1st Holy Comm

CONFIRMATION—Dinner @ Mayor's Restaurant in the Bronx

In the Kitchen—5th St. My Room on the
Left—Sisters Room to the Right

On 7th St. with Camille Immediato & her brother Carmine

Me in the Front

Wedding

Family Pix

First St. Joe's Grad

Names of 1st Grad

1st to graduate from New Church 1948
Graduated St. Joseph . 1948 ~ 49

Antoinette Ezzello
Lauccia Veltri
deline Boggi
Ellen Calicchio
ylvia La Tassa
(me) Joyce La Barbera
'nn Fontanarosa (Gibbons)
ary Schivone
ina Santora (Vera Amigion)
ie Stevenson

'aymond (Aloysia)
'e Carucato
Mary Anselem .

2nd Row
Joseph Giusi
Robert Amato
Thomas Tenuto
Sal Colangelo
John Cavaliere
Jim Sabia
Americo Colangeli
Vito Guglielmo
Vincent Sacco

4th Row
Anthony Buonsenino
Michael Veltri
John Rotz
Joseph Namie
Anthony Stevens
Anthony Bruno's
Sal Alofano Jr.
Patsy Marino
Joseph Pugliese
Anthony Lambido

3rd Row
Maryann Dos Reis
Connie De Masi (Touri
Antoinette Accocella
Barbara Bartucca
Eugene Gotti
Awelia Di Mardi
Isabelle Lovallo
Antonette Pinto
Marie Schippers (Pierro,

ST. JOSEPH'S CHURCH WASHINGTON AVENUE

More Names of Grad

St. Joseph Church grounds were always immaculate. The Shrubbery, the grass and of course the walkways and playground. As mentioned prior George Rainone who by trade and was self-employed as a landscaper volunteered of taking care of the landscape grounds.

The inside of the Church is beautiful as any church there is. The alter is gorgeous, the pews are of hard mahogany wood. The statues and architecture work is tremendous and of course the stain glass windows just phenomenal. The marble setting, the brass railings, the hanging chandelier lights, the candles all make the inside of St. Joseph Church a place of Holy Worship for the faith of the Catholic Religion—a making of self-inner soul for the love of God!

Before they came in with air condition they would have these huge big propeller type fans station from the alter to the rear of the church. At time in the dog days of the summer you would sit there or kneel and all you would hear would be the sound of the motor on those huge fans.

But the best sound was during the 9am Sunday mass that all the kids of the school had to attend and that was both St. Joseph Kids and the Columbus school relig kids (like myself). That sound was the cricket click made by the nun telling you when to stand, kneel or sit. And baby you better had obey those cricket sounds because if you didn't when you went to class you got more then that cricket sound was made of!!!!

I remember so vividly the sound of the church bells on Sunday that rung out for mass since we only lived down the block from the church.

The bells were always a wonderful peaceful joyous sound!

The sound of the church bells of a funeral rang out through out the neighborhood always with such a sad sound as they rang slow with the same tone. When the funeral procession drove by the neighbors would stop what they were doing and watch and pray as the hearse and casket went by so very slowly.

Wedding days were so wonderful, joyous and fun at St. Joseph Church. Everyone would love to throw rice as the married couple exited the church. People would bring boxes of "Carolina" rice and pour it into everyone's hands as we waited for the couple to come down the church steps to their waiting limo.

Everyone knew each other so it was common to stand in front of the church to watch someone from the neighborhood getting married even if you weren't invited to the reception.

As a kid you would throw rice at the bride and groom like you were throwing a baseball. If you ran out of rice you would bend down and scoop the rice off the steps and throw again!

But of course as you got a little older you kind of chucked the rice up in the air to land on both of them in a joyous manner in the celebration of their marriage.

The same went for funeral's, you didn't have to be a personal friend of the family. But as I said everyone knew each other or knew of them. You may not socialize on a daily basis but you knew who lived where and what street they lived on. So when someone passed away you might not have gone to the wake at Cancro's Funeral Parlor but you might have attended the mass of the deceased for the respect of your neighbor even though you didn't know them personally.

That's just the way it was in the "West."

CHAPTER (9)

"Feeney Park Boy's Club"

Anyone from the "West" sure has some wonderful memories of the Boy's Club. It could be about anyone or anything. Starting with August E. "Gus" Mascaro who I remember was the Executive Director for so many years. Of course Hank DeClemente known as "Hank-Deck" was the long time Unit Director who was just prolific and so much of a institution figure in the lives of us kids growing up in the 60's. Hank walked around with his little hat on just whistling and keeping an eye on the activities and each and every kid that walked and played through the doors of Feeney Park Boys Club.

In my day the club was used by boys only except for Friday night roller skating and then Saturday afternoon roller skating for the younger kids. Talking about Friday night skating. That was so much joy in everyone's life. We used to wait on line to get in. We would get their early so we can get our skates on and get on the gym floor as quick as we can. If you didn't have your own skates you would rent them and there would be volunteers to put them on for you in the corner of the gym. Of course if you were lucky to get a pair of your own skates you would go to the back little room just off the gym and put your skates on. I got my own boot style of skates from my sister, she gave me her skates so my mother dyed them black as boys had black and the girls had white boot skates.... *It worked for me!*

In my day I remember Jerome "Jerry" Valente very much involved with the Boy's Club activates especially the skating program. I remember very well Grace and Danny Grosso like some Olympic ice skaters around the gym so gracefully (no pun intended)—Others involved with the skating program were Charlie Brewer, Larry Rose, Sam Branca and Gary Figlutsie.

Feeney Park B.C.

THE CAST

Feeney Park Boy's Club Roller Skating Show (Cast)

My Boy's Club Skating Trophy I Won
Skating with Susan Samela—1963

To this day I still have my trophy I won with Susan Samela as a skating couple along with this writing pen they gave us both.

Tony DiPippo, Larry Rose and Jerry Valante are the adults I remember that were very instrumental with the hardball and softball programs when I was growing up. I'm sure there were a lot more that were involved since the community neighborhood either came to watch, volunteer or partake in the Boy's Club baseball programs and activities.

The old Boy's Club was remodeled and I have to say the first time I went back to the Club which was now utilized by both the "Boy's & Girl's I was a little dismayed to what I found. I just love the old gymnasium with the huge stage and the balcony over looking the gym activities. But that was all taken away with the new "Club." That balcony was great for viewing gym activities not to mention it was also utilized for activities while basketball games were going on. I can remember all the floor mats on the balcony taking tumbling lessons and other exercise work outs.

Sal Petrillo

When I was first going to the Boy's Club in the late 50's I was about 7 or 8 years old I can remember the old Rock n Roll Shows that were put on by the older kids at the time in the Boy's Club Gym. I remember Bruce Buono singing and dancing on that huge stage. I can remember a guy nicknamed "Crowbar" pounding the drums. Another singer Skip Giaco and a guitar player that looked like "Elvis" named Sal Petrillo who by the way walked around the "West" with his guitar on his back. Then their was a guy with the same last name as mine named Lewis Nardone who had a great voice. I'm sure there are many more but that is all I remember. I wish I could remember the guy who blew the sax he was sensational!

In the summer the Boy's Club had a wonderful "Day-Camp" program that was attended by a good majority of the kids in the neighborhood. A very affordable program that had Peter Acocella as the Camp Director. Mr. "Ack" was a Physical Education Teacher at Isaac E. Young Junior High School. I later played basketball and baseball for him when I attended IEY.

We would meet in the gym early in the morning for roll call and attendance. We were grouped off in groups and named after an Indian Tribe. The older boys from the club were counselors. We did all those camp activities and if it rained we stayed in the club all day.

They had a lot of arts & crafts activities as I remember. We made all those keys chains with the different colored plastic lace. They came on those big rolls and we would do the different weaving like a "Boxed" weave or the "Barrel" weave. They were great little gifts to mom & dad. We also did a lot of pottery work.

After we ate our lunch a bus would take us to Orchard Beach for a swim.

Once a week Mr. Ack would BBQ these foot long hot dogs at Orchard Beach. On BBQ day it was an all day affair. Those hot dogs were so crunchy and juicy as they stuck out on each end of the bun. *Soooo goooood!*

Then Mr. Ack would top off our hot dogs with these big slice's of watermelon and of course we as kids would be spitting the black pits at each other.

At the end of camp we would have all kinds of contests to win trophies. From basketball to softball to running track or just being a good kid!

I remember when I was about 10 years old and joined the boxing program. I don't remember who the trainers were. But it was funny as I think back at it. They would roll out the gray old dusty mats and then they put these huge 16oz boxing gloves on us. Then they would put these oversized head protector rotten leather (that smelled of old mildew) head gear on us that never fit right. So now your fighting, trying to punch the other kid and you can't see because the head gear is moving around your head and blocking your vision so your spending more time trying to move the head gear back into place and then Bam you get hit and your ass is on the mat!

But we did learn the art on how to stand, how to hold your hands and protect your face and body. To jab and all the other punching techniques and of course how to defend and so on.

There were so many programs at the Boy's Club besides the baseball/softball and skating programs. Basketball was a very big part of the club. On Saturday mornings the gym would be jammed with kids. After school in the cold months you ran to the club, throw your jacket on the stage to get a ball and basket first for a game or to shoot around of "21" or "Horse" or "Around the World" or just see who could make the most foul shots in a row. When we got bored we would challenge each other to some "wild-crazy" shots like from half court or some type of hook shot or go on the balcony and try and hit a basket from the balcony!

At the club we would go to the back room on the first floor past the locker room or go upstairs and play some pool or just hang out on the balcony of the gym!

Playing pool was also a big part of going to the Boy's Club. We would learn our art there as youngsters and then when we got a little older we would take a pool game to "Nick's Pool Hall" or to Larchmont the old "Executive Pool Lounge."

Of course we had the room where you could play checkers, chess and some other board games or as some other kids would start to learn their craft of playing "Cards"—Arts & Crafts was a program like they had from the camp days—Making key chains, pottery, finger painting, paper cut outs and other items for kids that liked working with their hands in a relaxing mode. Me I was one for running around and hanging at the gym.

During the cold months and school year as I said the Boy's Club was the place to be. Spring and the Summers we were on the ball field, or on the playground so the Boy's Club was virtually closed down except for Day Camp. We also had the Recreation Program at Columbus School as I also mention with Nello Amori. During the winter the school gym was opened and Nello ran the after school and summer playground programs. On Wednesday's all the kids went to Columbus School gym because the Boy's Club was setting up the gym for Wednesday night Bingo.

So we as kids had a wide variety of physical activates to keep us busy and out of trouble from hanging out on the streets. If you weren't into sport activities you could always join the arts & crafts program or go to the Feeney Park Library.

The Boy's Club was a foundation in most everyone's growing up. You learn how to get along with one another. You learn the art of sport activities. You were taught and learned how to share and act towards other people in a sensitive but in a "youth & young adult" manner! Yes—kid around—joke around—horse around like all kids do and yes we had a fist fight once in awhile among ourselves but we had a sense of respect that Gus, Hank, Nello and our parents instilled in us as kids growing up in the "West" towards your peers, neighbors and friends.

CHAPTER 10

"Feeney Park & Library"

If someone asked me what do I remember most about "Feeney Park"—I would say the pavilion on top of the hill near the Library and sleigh riding down the hill towards Green Place in the winter.

Feeney Park is just a beautiful carved out stretch of land that wasn't overly huge but it had or I should say it still does have character and a wonderful serene sense of relaxation. Back in the 50's-60's it started as you walked into the park from the 7th St. entrance as you pass the Columbus School playground. To your left was the Feeney Park Library that was mostly used by the St. Joseph School students because they didn't have a library or a magnitude of books in the school. Columbus School had it's own library but after school most of the kids from St. Joe's utilized the Feeney Park Library to study or for reference material.

On the other side of the library facing the Boy's Club but up on the hill where these actual big long cement steps that lead to a cement sidewalk type of walkway. The walkway kind of weaved it's way all around the park that made it for a nice walk through the park leading out to Green Place and to the beautiful arcade double winding steps to Madeline Ave.

The big hang out was the pavilion that had a covering to shade you from inclement weather. That was the place as a teenager you hung out, talking, smoking and just being cool!

Eventually the pavilion lost its covering and when the library was destroyed so was the pavilion.

I remember the library as this old wooden building with wooden floors that creaked as you walked. If I remember they had a small stairway that lead to the second floor. They had these hard wooden tables that the students sat at to do homework or read.

The Feeney Park Library served it's purpose and was a main stay that included the Boy's Club and the park. I didn't use it much. As I said any reference to reading us kids at Columbus utilized our own school library. I did have a Feeney Park library card and would go to take a book out once and awhile. But not very often. As I mentioned the park library was most utilized by St. Joseph Students and adults in the West.

Back in the late 50's and 60's there was no such thing as playing ball in the park. It was strictly a passive park. Just walk or sit on a bench except for the teenagers hang-in in the pavilion.

But when it was winter and the snow came down Feeney Park felt and looked like the Grand Canyon, the neighborhood kids would grab there old wooden sleds with the raw iron legs that we would sand paper with to remove all the rust. The sleigh had it's movable steering grips for each hand as we guided our sleds down the hill and sleigh all the way to Green Pl.

You can either lay on the sled or sit on it and steer with your feet.

There was the huge big tree right in the middle of the park and you had to steer around that tree or else "BAM"!

The best is when we would do a train by hooking our feet into the other person's sled. We would go down the hill with 8 to 10 hooked sleds till they all kind of zigzagged and unhooked going all different ways. At times we would double up on a sled either sitting or laying down.

But it was great fun sleigh riding at Feeney Park where we would stay for hours and hours on end till the snow melted to the grass.

Chapter (11)

Names and Faces from the "West"

If you Google New Rochelle the "West End"—*it says:*
A small neighborhood loosely defined on the southern border by Metro North's New Haven Line, on the West by the border with Pelham, on the North by Sickles Ave and on the East by Memorial Highway. Most of the neighborhood sits on a hill, which in the early days of New Rochelle was known as "Dutch Hill", leading to the terminology of saying someone is *"From up the West End."*

The neighborhood is and has traditionally been home to one of the area's larger immigrant populations, with the Italian immigration coming from 1900 through the 1950's and more recently the Hispanic immigration coming from about 1985 through the present populations

A lot of the names of people from the "West" I have already mentioned in the previous ten chapters. So many people that were recognized for whatever the reason why they were part of the "West."

One name, well known is Joe "Biff" Bevilaqua. I remember him wearing thick eye glasses and wore sunglasses all the time. His name was for whatever reason was always the butt of many jokes. I didn't know Joe to well. But he was always around Union Ave or at the Park. *Everyone knew Joe "Biff" that's for sure!*

Another guy I haven't mentioned was "Jimmy the Blade"—
I Didn't know him but knew of him!

Judy Morgan from Uncle's Department store from Union Ave between 4th St. & 3rd St. was another name and face that always seemed to get mentioned or heard of in some sense.

It always seems that their faces were always in the crowd along with of course a few other people from the "West" that we will leave to the imagination. They all had some sort of character stature to themselves and I'm sure there are a few I would have forgotten about that you may surely know!

As I stated I mentioned a lot of names in the previous ten chapters but as I scan my mind around the "West" you always think of names in the certain area's of the "West"—*Like:*

First St.—The Lazzo family—Over on *Second St.* I think of Bombace—Bellontoni—Bonanno—DiLeo—Torichelli. Over on *Third St.* I think of Cassara immediately along with Starpoli—Calgi and DiNapoli (Tina and her wonderful daughters who took over "Cooney's"—Over on *Fourth St.* my mind wanders right away to Cancro's and all the stores along 4th St. Then over on my street, *Fifth St.* you think of two names that come to mind Rainone & Garito. As we focus on *Sixth St.* names like Circelli—Girardi & Burigo pop up. Then over on *Seventh St.* two names are attached to 7th St. Generoso & Parente. The *Eighth & Ninth* St. area there is Frasca—Mauro—Gallo families.

Down on *Lafayette Ave* I think of the Barone's, the Palazzo, the Giannotti's and Nicky Gerome. Over on *Washington Ave* how could you not think of the Colangelo family along with the Lantz family (Lantz name attached to Disney World characters)—The Colangelo's had their own street name as you go up the alley from Washington Ave. I also think of the Cesario family on Washington Ave. Over towards 8th St on Washington my good friend the Paganico family lived. You can't forget the Samela, Carpenzano and Burroni families from *St. John's Place* or the Vitulli's, Cacciola's and DeLuca's behind the park in the *Green Pl.* section. On *Union Ave* Amorsano—Italiano—Cappolino's—Guida's—Della-Donna's—Marciano—Telesco. Over on Sickles Ave/Madeline Ave area there are the Carino's—Strazza—Covello—Amori—Mecca families. On Lockwood Ave of course Doc Attisani....Other names that come to mind Piedmont's—Palumbo—Columbo—Charla—DeRaffele....The list can go on and on....*You reminisce in your mind and think of all the names that come to mind as you read my list!*

CHAPTER (12)

"Proud of our Elected Officials"

The "West" has had their share of prominently proud "Elected Officials." I mentioned briefly in Chapter 5 and wrote about former Mayor's Frank Garito and Len Paudano from the "West." These two fine gentleman demonstrated a very high value of professionalism with high regard towards the City as they represented yes, all of New Rochelle residents but mainly the residents of the "West"—but more importantly they came from the "West" and that my friends was a true taste of Italian/American patriotism to the Italians that came to the United States and migrated to the "West End" of New Rochelle.

This made the "West End" residents feel secure and proud to be Italian/American from the "West."

It showed the true meaning of hard work and what this Country, the United States of America stands for—

You can do and be who and whatever you want to be successful if you work hard and commit and dedicate yourself to your beliefs and faith.

My list of "Elected Officials" from the "West" is as follows:
Honorable Ronald Tocci
Honorable Frank Garito
Honorable Leonard Paduano
Honorable Joseph Fosina

Honorable Rocco Bellantoni
Honorable "Doc" Attisani
Honorable Michael Boyle
Honorable Louis Trangucci
Honorable Albert Tarantino
Honorable Salvatore Tocci
Honorable Joseph Pisani

The list of "Elected Officials" from the "West" starts with the one and only Gentleman, Patriot and Statesman Mr. Ronald Tocci.

The prolific and long time public servant and community activist with a strong perseverance towards the assistance for the veterans and troops who serve and have served in the United States Military.

Honorable Tocci is a veteran having served in the military from 1966 to 1968 as a paratrooper in the Vietnam War.

His Political career started by serving as a County Legislator for the Westchester County Board of Legislature's from 1975 to 1984.

He then went on to serve as an Assemblyman in the New York State Assembly from 1985 to 2004.

Upon his retirement from the Assembly he was appointed as Deputy Commissioner for the Veterans Affairs for the NYS Department of Labor by then NYS Governor George Pataki.

Ron as a friend or acquaintance or the fine public servant he is always lend an ear, a hand and his generosity of public knowledge and experience to guide and assist anyone with a problem or event.

Ron is amazingly there for everyone at anytime and anywhere for so many many years!

Thank You Ron!

Garito

The Honorable Frank J. Garito served as Mayor for the City of New Rochelle from 1970 till 1976. Prior to that he served with the Westchester County Board of Supervisors.

Frank served in the United States Army during the Korean War with the rank of Sergeant.

I knew Frank, his wife and three children very well as they lived at 17 Fifth Street while I was growing up at 9 Fifth Street....

Always a Gentleman, a true Family Man. A Terrific Neighbor and true to his Faith.

Frank was one of the finest human beings that New Rochelle ever had. A man without a true education that worked hard with the family business the "James Garito & Sons" contracting company and then later starting his own business with his family.

Frank loved his Country, he loved New Rochelle, he loved his family and he loved people and people loved Frank!

Tall—Dark and debonair they said about Frank who married his high school sweetheart Rose—Frank worked ten hour days and at night he went to wakes, meetings or anywhere that served his will to help and improve the quality of life for his immediate neighbors, the many organizations he belonged too or the New Rochelle residents at large.

Len on the Radio - WVOX   Len as a Speaker

The Honorable Leonard Paduano, another terrific and proud Elected Official from the "West" that so many of us are happy to have known for so many years. Another gentleman who dedicated himself to serving and doing whatever he can for the residents of New Rochelle. An honest "Abe" type of guy with a high standard of integrity—Len is a very bright man with a wealth of knowledge and understanding of the meaning of community and the effort of working together for the same goal for a City that could prosper with good hard working mechanics and mobility in a successful functioning manner so everyone may benefit for the better.

He believed in progress and moving forward to thrive for a better New Rochelle in all aspects of life.

Len served as Mayor of New Rochelle from 1980 to 1991.

The rest of the list "Elected Officials" encounters a wide variety of men who all had or have (time of this writing two councilman are still serving) the same goal and determination in mind. That is to make the best choices for the city to improve the quality of life, to keep essential services in place. To keep taxes down and in a affordable alliance with the economy. To make choices to improve conditions for infrastructure and always improve the environment. To enjoy the best of parks and recreation. To improve the Main St. and shopping area's in the City....The bottom line, keep New Rochelle improving and moving forward, to keep it safe, family oriented, diverse and one of the finest Cities in Westchester, the State and Country to live and work.

Honorable Joseph F. Fosina, community minded hard working New Rochelle individual elected and served as City Councilman and as everyone knows a very good friend of Mariano Rivera of the NY Yankees. So many articles have been written about Joe & Mo. Joe was raised in the "West End" on Lockwood Ave between 4th St. and Madeline Ave. Mr. Fosina was part owner of "Glen Sport Shop" located up on Union Ave by the Casa Calabria Society Club. I purchased my first Little League Cleats there.

He has many years of being in charge of the NY Yankees uniforms—cleaning—tailoring etc—pick up and delivery....Mr. Fosina has been very instrumental with the Youth Tackle Football Leagues for over 35 years. In his name and deservingly so the new athletic fields in City Park off Fifth Ave were named in his honor for all the many years as president and involved with YTL as a very successful program for the youth of New Rochelle.

Honorable Rocco Bellantoni Jr. political leader from the "West End" and served as New Rochelle City Councilman. A man of a few business's but ever so known for Bellantoni's Deli at the bottom of the hill of Second St opposite Jones St.

A giving man for so many charities who was well respected not only in the "West" but beyond the boundary lines of "West" New Rochelle!

Honorable D. Anthony "Doc" Attisani served the community in various capacities. Starting as the City Marshall for New Rochelle for 12 years, then as Westchester County Supervisor (Legislator) for 4 terms and then as Chief Court Clerk for New Rochelle for over 10 years. Doc Attisani was educated in the New Rochelle School System then graduated from Iona College and received a Doctorate from Columbia Institute of Chiropractics.

Dr. Attisani a brilliant mind also served in the U.S. Navy from 1942-1946. He completed the V-12 Program at Oberlin College, Central Michigan College and Notre Dame Midshipman School. He was an ensign during WWII.

Honorable Michael Boyle—served on the New Rochelle Council as a Councilman in the South End. Mr. Boyle also a very bright person is a teacher by trade. He served his community well and could of stayed on to win a few more elections but decided to commit to other obligations. Mr. Boyle is from the Van Guilder Ave section of New Rochelle.

Honorable Louis Trangucci—Watching this young man grow up and eating a sausage & peppers hero with Ernie Viccaro on Union Ave I'm personally proud to see and observe as he serves his community so well. Lou loves the "West" and New Rochelle. A product of the New Rochelle School System and a grad of Iona College with a degree in Business. Lou is a dedicated family man, a dedicated Civil Servant. Always there to volunteer his services from the Memorial Day Parade to the Feast at St. Joseph.

At the writing of this book Mr. Trangucci is serving on the New Rochelle Council in District #1.

Honorable Albert Tarantino born on St. John's Place but grew up in the Van Guilder Ave section of New Rochelle. I remember vividly from the teenage days of Al swimming in the pool of the Cacciatore household or partaking at the Feeney Park Boy's Club activities. During the writing of this book Mr. Tarantino is currently serving as a Councilman for the City of New Rochelle.

Councilman Tarantino served in the U.S. Air Force.

Mr. Tarantino is Co-owner of Talner Jewelers on Main St. in New Rochelle. A business that dates back to 1927. Talner Jewelers is one of the only remaining business's in the Main Street area from the glory days of the downtown district that was vibrant of so many various shopping stores.

A bright mind of business, always a gentleman and a person of the community. Mr. Tarantino has served as President of the New Rochelle Chamber of Commerce and as a member of the Board of Directors. Al is also a board member for (BID) Business Improvement District. Al also serves on the board for the Educational Excellence, the YMCA and the United Way of New Rochelle and also serves as a member of the New Rochelle Downtown Task Force. He is a former member of the New Rochelle Waterfront Advisory Committee and former member of the Sans Souci Homeowners Association as well as the Advisory Committee on Boating & Marinas.

Al always in tune with community activities with the residents of his district as well the rest of the New Rochelle Citizens. A true community activist in every sense of the word.

Honorable Salvatore Tocci who grew up on 4th Street between Washington Ave and St. John's Place from my understanding was the first resident of the "West End" to be elected in any capacity as an elected official serving with the Westchester County Board of Supervisors which eventually became the Board of Legislators. Mr. Tocci served from around 1945 and was elected to (7) 2 year terms.

I didn't know Sal Tocci personally but from what I heard he was very much respected and a loved person from the "West" as many of the Italians looked up to him for help, assistance and guidance in the struggling years of war time and while working to support the family.

Honorable Joseph R. Pisani, an attorney by trade served in the New York State Legislative Government first as a NYS Assemblyman then for nearly 20 years as a New York Senator. Known for many years as a Child and Disability Advocate fighting for the rights and for many bills of assistance for the disabled.

On a personal note I can honestly say the Senator Pisani was very instrumental in helping and assisting the needs of my brother who you read about earlier in the book.

CHAPTER (13)

"Holiday's in the Old Neighborhood"—"The West"

I can tell you now, nothing like the Holidays in the "West" in the late 50's and the 60's. I don't remember too much about New Year's Eve. For me on New Year's Day when I was in my young teens like 13-14-15 years old all I remember is my God-Father Nick Circelli and his wife Rose would come over to the house (called it a house but it was a 5 room apartment) for dinner. I sat and watched mostly the College Bowl Football games until everyone got tired of talking in the kitchen and made there way to the living room so football was over and some TV special got put on around 8pm. I usually knew it was time for the adults to make their way to the living room when I stopped hearing the nuts crack!

After the long winter and spring sprung it meant two things. Baseball and Easter. It meant getting out their and throwing the ball around. But for most the flowers and green grass was upon us as we all looked forward to a beautiful Easter Sunday. Of course leading up to Easter for us Catholics were lent and as always you would give up eating something for the time of lent. As you followed the religion there was Ash Wednesday, no eating of meat on Friday's, Holy Thursday, Good Friday and certain other religious days that you followed. But on Easter Sunday you would come outside and either before or after church everyone would be taking family pictures.

Little girls with their cute little dresses and bonnets, the boys in their new blue suit and if it was warm enough the little kids would be wearing a new suit with a style of short pants instead of long trousers. Families headed to see the Grand Parents and other family members. Back then most of your family including grandparents lived in the area so the neighborhood would be covered with everyone walking to someone else's home to wish them "Happy Easter."

Of course we all couldn't wait to get our Big Chocolate Bunny!

The next big Holiday was the 4th of July in the "West." I can't imagine how I can describe the 4th in the "West." First of all the fire-crackers or fire-works would start "booming" around the neighborhood at least two weeks prior. I mean you would hear them going off all day until about 11pm or so. Feeney Park and the hang out crowd had the park going Boom Boom Boom constantly! That's all you would hear till the 4th of July. *Boom Boom Boom!*

Back then the City held their annual fire-works display at New Rochelle High School by the twin lakes. That was a nice atmosphere because people would gather all around the lakes as the colorful rockets lit up the sky. But the parking was terrible (neighborhood parking) so eventually the site was moved to Five Island Park.

As I said I can't imagine how to describe the 4th of July because all of the neighborhood would head to Union Ave and 2nd Street. I could only describe it like a war zone. The Police would place barricades on the corners as the locals from Union Ave did their thing blasting every conceivable type of fire-works made!

Union Ave and 2nd Street. fire-work display would go on for at least 3 hours that I remember of constant blasting of fire-works. It was just an amazing display of illegal fire-work display that you had to witness to understand the magnitude of it all. Eventually the police said enough is enough and that would be the end as it got close to midnight.

As compared to today it was unbelievable the amount of fire-works that were in the neighborhood. Fire-Crackers, Cheery-Bombs, M-80's etc etc...Sky-Rockets of all types that burst in the air with the fancy colors. You name it you can get it and very affordable back then! We would buy what they called "A Brick" of Fire-Works and just walk around the neighborhood lighting off fire-works.

Yes, their was some crazy, foolish different ways of shooting off the fire-works. Like tying a few M-80's together and throwing them in a metal garbage can and placing the lid on top and then "Wham' that lid would go flying! Placing them in trees till the branch would go flying. Throwing them at cars and trains. Opening someone's front door and throwing a fire-cracker in the hallway. And yes, *but not me* there were some very mean things done to animals with fire-crackers.

Anyway, just harmless teens celebrating the true meaning of the 4th of July.... *The Birth of our Great Country, the USA!*

As the summer ended and we went back to school the next Holiday we looked for was Halloween.

Prior to Halloween, the night before was always considered "Mischief Night"—A night of throwing eggs spraying everything with shaving cream!....Store owners were eventually told not to sell either product on that day to the youngsters....*I wonder why!*.... At Columbus Elementary School each class would have there Halloween party. Kids would wear their costume and the parents would bring in the cupcakes and the teachers would say "OK Class—No Homework today so you can go "Trick or Treating" in the Neighborhood"—"Be careful and remember what I told you about receiving candy—fruit and money!"—We would all say "Thank You Mrs. So & so" and run out the door. Each house would be decorated with lights and decorations of Halloween ornaments. The usual so-called scary creatures with grave stones and lit up Jack-O-Lanterns.

The mothers would go out "Trick or Treating" early while it was still light out with the very young little darlings. So cute they were in there little angel or devil costume.

Us 12-13teen year older kids would wait for the dark to fall and then hit the streets and houses.

By the door (and all doors were open then)—everyone would have a table with the little bags of candy for us and lots of people especially down over the Pelham-New Rochelle border line on Washington Ave the home-owners would throw a nice chunk of change in your Halloween bag. When your bag got full and it was still early enough to Trick or Treat we would run home empty the bag on the bed and run back out for more. We would eat a little candy here and there and constantly shake the bag to hear the coins rattle. If it rattled pretty good we knew we were having a good night!

When I was young mom would take me to Woolworth's on Main St. to get a Halloween costume. When you walked into Woolworth's they had all the costume's hanging from a wire from the ceiling. They were made of thin nylon material, they came with a mask (that you never wore as it always itched your nose and rubbed against your eyebrows.) After picking out my costume mom would take me over to the luncheonette counter and along the counter above you was a string of balloons. You would pick out a balloon and the counter lady would bust the balloon and find a little piece of paper in it and it would indicate the price of the banana split. It went from 1-cent to if I remember 69 or 89-cent.

As I got older I dumped the costume and just dressed up in some old rags and dungy clothes, painted my face with some black Halloween crayons and called myself a "hobo."

Thanksgiving another one of those special Holiday's for everyone up the "West." Do I need to tell you the festive Thanksgiving meal in the 50's-60's! Well if I have to, lol you must know there is not getting up from the table for a least 6 hours. Of course the traditional turkey with salad, soup, antipasti, another meat of some sort, lasagna, vegetables, stuffing from the turkey, all kinds of desserts, wine of your choice, after dinner drinks, nuts, fruit, candy etc.

Thanksgiving day started with the traditional New Rochelle High School vs. Iona Prep "Turkey Bowl" Football game. If you didn't make it to the game you watched it on Channel 11 on the television. Something that all the other high schools were jealous about. Can't say I don't blame them. But one of Channel 11 executives lived in the area so he profiled the traditional game each year.

When I got into my teens my brother in law who was a graduate of Cardinal Hayes High School in the Bronx would take me to the Hayes vs. Mt. Saint Michael football game on Thanksgiving morning.

In the schools and in the church we would bring cans of food, clothing for those a little less fortunate. There were the neighbors that would volunteer their time at some local soup kitchens.

On T.V. there were the NFL football games and usually a double header of NBA basketball as well.

After dinner the guys plummeted their butts in the living room for a rest and watch some football, the ladies cleaned up a little and then it was back to the table.

Thanksgiving dinner usually meant anywhere from 10 to 40 for dinner.

Mom & Dad would prepare the turkey the night before and then my dad would get up about 6-7am and place it in the oven to start cooking it.

After a few years Dad would take the turkey over to the Marciano bakery early in the morning and they would cook it in their huge oven.

Thanksgiving was also the start of the Christmas Holiday season. The vibrant Main St. area of New Rochelle was gearing up for the Holiday season sales. Bloomingdales, Arnold Constable, Grants, Woolworths, Sears, Mendolsons, Toy stores, Frost Mens Shop, the Army & Navy stores, Caruso Music Store, Hardware stores, Bicycle shops and more. The Main St luncheonette's were busy with shoppers, The movie theaters, RKO, Loew's, Town theater busy with tired shoppers. Then on the Thursday night before Thanksgiving it was the Thanksgiving Parade in New Rochelle. Cold but festive and fun for the whole community! The conclusion of the parade would always have Santa on top of the New Rochelle Fire Truck.

Let the Christmas Season begin!

In the "West" the neighbors were already decorating their outside homes with Christmas Lights, ornaments as the Holiday Season was as I stated beginning. Everyone would get their Christmas tree from the corner of Washington Ave and Webster Ave. Time to go to the attic or the cellar (as we called it then) and unwind all the wires and Christmas light bulbs. Clean off the bulbs and see what tinsel was still usable.

On T.V. it was time for all the Christmas specials. Perry Como Christmas Special, Dean Martin Special, Johnny Mathis Christmas Special. All the Christmas movies like "It's A Wonderful Life"—"White Christmas"

On the Radio we were listening to "Dominick the Donkey"—"Rockin Around the Christmas Tree—"White Christmas"—"Jingle Bell Rock" of course all the traditional songs. Still very popular was "Volare" and "That's Amore"—In school we had the Christmas Choir Festivals.

Yes Christmas time in the "West" was very special especially at St. Joseph Church. Always decorated so festive. The huge green wreath hanging in front of the church. The altar decorated with the red and white poinsettias plants.

When it was time for us Catholic's to attend confession at the church to report our sins to the priest the church would have very long lines around the church waiting to go into the confession box. As you enter the box you could hear vaguely the priest speaking with the other person and when he was ready for you the little window would slide open as you were kneeling in the dark little closet setting. You would start your prayer and then the priest would ask you for what sins do you wish to have forgiven from your soul. After reporting your sins to the priest he would direct you your penance of prayer and you would go to the altar and pray on the amount of different prayers the priest assigned to you to say. You were now forgiven of your sins from the Lord. You were now able to receive the Holy Eucharist at Christmas Mass.

Christmas Eve in the "West End" of New Rochelle—You can smell the aroma of fish, the marinara simmering in the large pots with clam or lobster sauce. Spaghetti or Linguini ready to cook Aldente style. The frying of cod fish (Baccala), mussels, clams, squid, scallops and so on in all the neighborhood made it a festive family oriented fun time in a religious manner. The annual tradition of "Christmas Eve" dinner celebrating the "Midnight Birth of Baby Jesus." They called it the celebration of the 7 fishes but it wasn't uncommon for some households to eat 9—11—13 other different fish. Pasta, vegetables were included in your meals.

Some families opened Christmas presents before midnight mass, some opened presents after midnight mass. It all depended on who was going elsewhere on Christmas Day to visit family and friends.

Midnight Mass at St. Joseph church was filled to capacity. To handle the large crowd of people attending mass the overflow of worshipers had to attend midnight mass in the church hall that was used as an annex of midnight mass. On your way to mass and at the conclusion of mass the neighborhood was filled with people hugging, kissing, shaking hands as everyone wished each other a very "Merry Christmas."

If we were lucky we would have a little snow to really have a Norman Rockwell type of Christmas!

Christmas morning in the "West"—You woke up with Holiday spirit enthusiasm. You have that religious faith in you and you have the family traditional Christmas spirit of giving. Every family did their own style of celebrating. If you didn't make it to midnight mass you then went to church in the morning. Neighbors and friends were out early making early visits to wish everyone a "Merry Christmas" before you went visiting or the family and friends were part of your Christmas dinner. Either way, the joyous occasion of Holiday spirit was in the air in the "West"—It was one happy celebration because the "West" was like one big happy family!

In the afternoon on Christmas day, after opening of presents and the kids playing with their new toys or some kid outside riding his new 3 speed bicycle. Maybe trying out the new football or baseball glove it was time for the afternoon Christmas feast. While coming off the Christmas Eve dinner it didn't matter because Christmas Eve and Christmas day were two different meals and you sat with family and friends as we still do but back in the 50's and 60's it's just a little bit more special as you were growing up.

We hope the tradition stayed in your family as a lot of people moved to different sections of New Rochelle other towns or even out of state. But as you grew up in the 50's-60's and you had children and met new friends I hope the foundation of growing up back then continued the love and joyous feeling of the Christmas spirit both traditional and with the Lord in mind.

Yes, it was not all Catholic's and Italians in the "West"—Black Americans, people of Jewish faith and others but it didn't matter we were all "family" if you lived in the "West End" of New Rochelle in the 50's-60's

Don't take this personal: celebrate or don't celebrate—your wish: But: Keep the "Christ" in Christmas—"Merry Christmas"

Chapter (14)

"Junior & High School Years"

My High School years started for me with going to Isaac E. Young Junior High School for 7th—8th and 9th grades. Then making the transition of going to New Rochelle High School for 10th—11th and 12th. "IEY" located on the corner of Centre Ave and Pelham Rd and the first thing you think of is wow elementary school was up the block now I have to go cross town to get to school. "No school buses then" only the "P" Webster bus that you stopped on the corner of Union Ave and 4th St. You then walked the rest of the way down Centre Ave to the School. Dad did drive me once in awhile or at least dropped me off at Centre and Main St. or you just got your butt in gear and walked from the "West" to "IEY"—*Whatever way but you got there.*

Isaac E. Young, the school that looks like a castle. All of a sudden as a student your walking from one class to another. You have a school locker in the hallway for your books. Your now going to gym class and changing your clothes on a time schedule and taking showers in front of strangers. All of a sudden it's not 95% Italians in your class. Jewish, Irish, Anglo-Saxon's, more Black-African Americans, some Spanish. Now your meeting new friends from the south end of the city, east side of the city. Now your seeing more girls and more boys.

Teenage/adolescent life is in full swing for all of us. A whole new world is opening up, a whole new dimension of different personalities and life styles. How do we juggle this lifestyle change of getting back and forth to school that's on the other side of the City, Meeting all these new faces. Different teachers for each class, not one teacher each day as we were use to. Loads of homework! A new challenge, a whole new change with the guidance of parents, family and friends you embrace it all and meet the challenge head on and accept the fact your new life style! Comb your hair more, Wash more, dress a little neater and learn a little more about life and your new education studies.

Of course now girls came into our lives. Girls from the south and east end of town, not that we didn't have pretty cute girls from the "West" we sure did but they were girls we grew up with and after a while they would feel like your sister by the time you got to 13 years old.

I don't know what happened to Danny Costa at IEY, but I do know he started learning his trade as a master mechanic while working after school in local car repair shops. Mauro was still at St. Joseph so I didn't see much of him until he came over to IEY as he entered 9th grade. But we would get together on Saturday's and I would tell him all about IEY and the girls that were there and how school was so different going to different classes and different teachers. We would go to Main St. for the Woolworth's balloon banana split and then go over to Hardy Shoes that was located on the corner of Main St. and Division St. One day we bought our "New Style"—"Square Toe" shiny black shoes. Mauro loved those shoes he would shine them to a mirror. He would walk down the street just looking down on those shoes looking from side to side making sure their were no scuff marks. If there were, he would buff it out and polish those shoes to make them look new again and that is a true story. But Mauro like the rest of us when we found out there was a world outside the "West" and then found girl's he, like us all as I said prior, washed a little more, dressed a little better etc.

After Hardy's then it was over to Caruso's Music Store on Main St near Centre Ave across the street from the RKO Movie Theater to check out the new release records and just gaze up at all the drums and guitars all over the store. Caruso's was a wonder world of Music. The "House of Music" music store was down the street by Loew's Theater but it was nothing like Caruso's. House of Music had a lot of 45 records and sheet music but Caruso's had the instruments galore all over the store from the ceiling to the floor and all the latest equipment.

Yes, 7th and 8th grades were sure more of the formative or adolescent years as we start to work out with weights. For myself playing more team sports for Nello's basketball team on Saturday mornings. At night I got hooked up with John Cacciatore, Phil DeRaffele and Tommy Delfico as myself and Joey Morello from the south side were asked to play on their night recreation basketball team.

I met Joey Morello in 7th grade homeroom and we kind of hit it off as friends right away as we both weren't the best of school work candidates and we both loved sports.

The Jets and Joe Namath were flying high, Joey was a big Namath guy. During lunch and little after school Joe and I would hook up in some good ole touch football games in the area. Joe could have been a very good High School Quarterback but didn't get a real break on the IEY freshman football team. Joey was always the QB as he threw to me. Joey and I remained friends for the three years at IEY. I hung out with his friends in the south end playing baseball & softball. By the time it was time to go to the High School as usual things change. Joey went on to do some boxing and eventually went into the service. To this day, I remember back in the late 60's Joey was home on leave and he said to me "Dennis the Mid-East part of the World is going to change everything the way we live some day."—Wow was he right!

Back in the "West Side" after meeting Johnny Cacc, Tommy Delfico and Phil DeRafflele myself and Mauro began a whole new friendship with these guys. "Johnny Cacc" (as we called him) lived on Van Guilder Ave, Phil in Edgewood Park and Tommy lived up on Badeau Place by Washington School and the top of Union Ave just before Memorial Highway and the Main St. area.

With those guys came Ernie Fossa and Sal DeRaffele (no relation to Phil), Ken Perrotti, Paul Shelton, Bill Lauer and then Gary Lisk and Jack DeRosa.

Catching Baseball

In 9th grade while on the IEY baseball team with Ernie. My claim to fame was saving Ernie's No-Hitter as he was pitching a gem. I was playing first base for Coach Pete Acocella's team and all of a sudden a screaming line drive was hit down the first base line and I was able to nab it and save Ernie's No-Hitter.

Phil DeRaffele was the son of Mr. Phil DeRaffele who is President of DeRaffele Diners Corporation. Johnny Cacciatore's mom is a DeRaffele.

As we entered New Rochelle High School. It sure was a "Wonder World" trying to find your way from one side of the school to the other side. It was just an amazing feat. I'm sure anyone that entered the halls and classrooms of NRHS knows what I am speaking about because until you learned your way around you got lost in the halls very easy.

By then our looks started to change, no more slick back greaser hair cuts, we let our hair down with the Beatle, Beach Boy hair style. Sandals, jeans, no socks and what they called the "Collegiate Look"—The summer was all day at the beach's. Hudson Park but mostly sneaking into Beach & Tennis to hang out with Phil and John who where members.

By time we entered the 11th grade it was growing our hair long, bell bottoms, tie-dyed shirts all that 60's good stuff.

I was also working part time at Daylight Meateria on Main St. near Caruso's Music Store slicing cold-cuts. I then went to work at Cambridge University Press on North Ave across the street from New Rochelle City Hall.

The barber shops up the "West" went from giving hair cuts to "Styling Hair Cuts" to try to keep up with making a living as the hair cuts got less and less with the younger generation.

Viccaro's Restaurant was still the best for pizza and sausage & pepper wedges. Mario's Pizza on Washington Ave was making a name for themselves with their pizza and food as well.

The biggest event of my junior year at New Rochelle High School was of course the tragic School fire that burned down much of the school. It was May of 1968. The rest of the school year was a mess of things as we had to finish the school year at Albert Leonard Junior high School. Most of the time we hung out in the muddy fields that was used as the parking lot for students and teachers. Most of our final exams were cancelled except for college regents.

A few weeks prior, fires were set all of the time in waste baskets or lockers and alarms were going off all the time.

I found out later that I was a possible suspect in the investigation who might have started the fire that burned the school down.

My father used to drive me to the High School very early because he had to get to work. He always left me off in front of the auditorium and I would be the first student on the steps and ironically my locker was upstairs where the fire started. I was later told by my health teacher Mr. Frank Lombardo who said "No Way Dennis could be involved". While they were looking for me to talk with me, myself along with some friends jumped on the train and went to NYC when they announced school was cancelled for the day. We all thought it was going to be another little fire and it would be put out like the fires that were happening for the last couple of weeks.

When we returned on the train we heard people talking that New Rochelle High School had burned down.

We all freaked out on that train returning to New Rochelle in disbelief feeling terrible about what we heard!

They caught the fire bug when he tried to burn down Albert Leonard!

No-Hitter For Fossa
In 5-0 Young Victory

Friday the 13th proved no jinx for young Ernie Fossa as he fird a no-hitter for Isaac E. Young Junior High School in a 5-0 victory over Cardinal Spellman's freshmen at Trinity Field yesterday.

Fossa struck out nine in his route-going stint over seven frames. Spellman got five base runners, all on walks.

Willie Ozzie, Jan Goldsmith ??? Frank Puglia scored for the Knights in the 2d and with Josh Bogin aboard in the 3d, Ozzie drilled a long home run.

Dennis Nardone and Puglia each spiked two hits for the victors, who totaled nine off Bullets Blanco.

Friday, The 13th: Really Bad Luck?

"**Mr. Santora,** could you please let me off here. I want to go tell them (the baseball team) how we slaughtered **Harrison** 94-15 in the track meet. Wait till **Hymie** hears this!" (**Hymie**, or **Bruce Hochberg**, was the **Castle Courier** reporter at the scene of the game against **Cardinal Spellman**.) I ran through the gate at **Trinity Field** and up to the players bench where **Hymie** was scoring. I was all set to tell him of the track win when he whispered something that had me flabbergasted. "**Schwartz**," he said, "**Ernie (Fossa)** hasn't allowed any hits." He's pitching a no-hitter!!!

—Suspense—

I sat down and surveyed the situation. We were ahead 5-0, on a two-run homer by **Ozzie Wille** after **Josh Bogin** had tripled. It was now the seventh inning. Three more outs and Ernie would have it. I picked my head up just in time to see the **Spellman** batter hit a high, hard bouncer down the first base line to **Dennis Nardone. Dennis** fielded it and stepped on first. One out. **Ernie** got ahead of the next batter as the man swung at the first two pitches. Now I expected a high inside fastball, as this is the way **Coach Acocella** usually pitches on 0-2 count. A swing and a miss. Two out. The next man walked on 5 pitches. **Bob Flood,** the catcher, took his time with the ball as he tried to relax **Ernie.** Shouts of encouragement came from our bench cheering the team on. Most of the bench, **Mr. Ac** and **Delvecchio,** and the spectators were standing, as the first pitch, a blazing fast ball went to the plate. Strike one! A cheer came up from the crowd. Next a curve. Low, ball one. This time shouts of encouragement came with the call. Another curve. Strike two! It was one of those real beauties you could see break, and as it did a moan came up from the **Spellman** bench. Everyone was set to rush out on the field on the next pitch. But not just yet. This time the curve was slightly inside. The count was 2-2. Now every eye was on **Ernie.** You could see him reach back for something extra as he threw his fastball. A swing and a miss! The game was over! He had done it! As soon as the man swung, pandemonium broke loose. The entire pitcher's mound was covered by players and well wishers alike. In his one man show, **Ernie** struck out 9, walked only 5, knocked in 2 runs with a single, and on Friday the 13th yet!!!. This game can be summed up with just four words. **Ernie Fossa,** powerful stuff!!!!

HS Fire

Left to Right—
Al Tarantino—Gary Lisk—Me—Phil DeRaffele—(?)—Ernie Fossa

No-Hitter For Fossa
In 5-0 Young Victory

Friday, the 13th proved no jinx for young Ernie Fossa as he fired a no-hitter for Isaac E. Young Junior High School in a 5-0 victory over Cardinal Spellman's freshmen at Trinity Field yesterday.

Fossa struck out nine in his route-going stint over seven frames. Spellman got five base runners; all on walks.

Willie Ozzie, Jan Goldsmith Frank Puglia scored for

the Knights in the 2d and with Josh Bogin aboard in the 3d, Ozzie drilled a long home run.

Dennis Nardone and Puglia each spiked two hits for the victors, who totaled nine off Bullets Blanco.

Friday, The 13th:
Really Bad Luck?

"**Mr. Santora**, could you please let me off here. I want to go tell them (the baseball team) how we slaughtered **Harrison** 94-15 in the track meet. Wait till

Hymie hears this!" (Hymie, or **Bruce Hochberg**, was the **Castle Courier** reporter at the scene of the game against **Cardinal Spellman**.) I ran through the gate at **Trinity Field** and up to the players bench where **Hymie** was scoring. I was all set to tell him of the track win when he whispered something that had me flabbergasted. "**Schwartz**," he said, "**Ernie (Fossa)** hasn't allowed any hits." He's pitching a no-hitter!!!

—Suspense—

I sat down and surveyed the situation. We were ahead 5-0, on a two-run homer by **Ozzie Wille** after **Josh Bogin** had tripled. It was now the seventh inning. Three more outs and **Ernie** would have it. I picked my head up just in time to see the **Spellman** batter hit a high, hard bouncer down the first base line to **Dennis Nardone**. **Dennis** fielded it and stepped on first. One out. **Ernie** got ahead of the next batter as the man swung at the first two pitches. Now I expected a high inside fastball, as this is the way **Coach Acocella** usually pitches on 0-2 count. A swing and a miss. Two out. The next man walked on 5 pitches. **Bob Flood**, the catcher, took his time

with the ball as he tried to relax **Ernie**. Shouts of encouragement came from our bench cheering the team on. Most of the bench, **Mr. Ace** and **Delvecchio**, and the spectators were standing, as the first pitch, a blazing fast ball went to the plate. Strike one! A cheer came up from the crowd. Next a curve. Low, ball one. This time shouts of encouragement came with the call. Another curve. Strike two! It was one of those real beauties you could see break, and as it did a moan came up from the **Spellman** bench. Everyone was set to rush out on the field on the next pitch. But not just yet. This time the curve was slightly inside. The count was 2-2. Now every eye was on **Ernie.** You could see him reach back for something extra as he threw his fastball. A swing and a miss! The game was over! He had done it! As soon as the man swung, pandemonium broke loose. The entire pitcher's mound was covered by players and well wishers alike. In his one man show **Ernie** struck out 9, walked only 5, knocked in 2 runs with a single, and on Friday the 13th yet!!! This game can be summed up with just four words. **Ernie Fossa** powerful stuff!!!!

Prom

HS Pix

NEW ROCHELLE HIGH SCHOOL

Adolf Panitz .... *Principal*
Harold A. Daley .... *Assistant Principal*
Raymond C. Schenk .... *Assistant Principal*
Helene C. Jenkins .... *Dean of Girls*
Ira Sarton .... *Dean of Boys*
George H. Eckels .... *Principal Emeritus*
F. Loretta Coons .... *Principal Emerita*

SENIOR COUNSELORS

Dorothy Curran   Loretta D. Smythe
Robert Kenney   Calvin Wintman
Rick F. Yacone

SOCIAL ADVISER FOR THE CLASS OF 1969
Thomas M. Walsh

BOARD OF EDUCATION
James K. Bishop, *President*

Raymond D. Galof   James Dandry
Mrs. Arthur Carol   Stanley H. Gould, D.D.S.
Frank H. Connelly   George S. Hills
Mrs. Howard B. Kane

George C. Clark, *Superintendent of Schools*

Seventy-fourth

Graduation Exercises

OF

NEW ROCHELLE HIGH SCHOOL

Class of 1969

Held at NEW ROCHELLE HIGH SCHOOL

NEW ROCHELLE, NEW YORK

SUNDAY, JUNE THE TWENTY-SECOND

NINETEEN HUNDRED SIXTY-NINE

PROGRAM

Processional March from "Athalia" .... Mendelssohn
New Rochelle High School Band
Salute to the Flag .... *Class and Audience*
Led by Jonathan Edward Barnes
"The Star-Spangled Banner" .... *Class and Audience*
Scripture Reading .... Dr. George M. Davis, Jr.
Address of Welcome .... Eric Herman Vinton
Address .... Peter J. Sims
Valedictorian
"Trumpet in the Night" .... Harold Simeone
Soloist — Charles Morgan LeCount, Jr.
New Rochelle High School Band
The Class of 1969 .... Adolf Panitz
Principal, New Rochelle High School
Presentation of the Class of 1969 .... George C. Clark
Superintendent of Schools
Acceptance of the Class of 1969 .... James K. Bishop
President, Board of Education
Presentation of Diplomas .... James K. Bishop
Alma Mater .... *Class and Audience*
*Recessional March —"Minute Man" .... Robert Pearson
New Rochelle High School Band

ALMA MATER

Joan Ronder '43   Jerry Cole '43

New Rochelle, we sing to thee,
Alma Mater dear.
Cherished will our mem'ries be
Of the hours spent here.
We love to gaze across the lake
To the tower proudly high,
A symbol of the lives you make,
The goals for which we try.

*The audience is requested to remain in place until the entire Class of 1969 has left the field.

NATIONAL MERIT SCHOLARSHIP FINALISTS

Donald Bruce Alpert
Alan Jeffrey Auerbach
Julie Blatt
Steven Goldfinger
Arnold Gordon
Frederick Sanford Harris
Linda Miriam Yowell

NATIONAL MERIT SCHOLARSHIP — LETTERS OF COMMENDATION

Rita Belserene
Terry G. Bergman
Joshua Paul Bogin
Peter Israel Breger
Barbara Ann Bruce
Robin Chalek
Barbara Dorfman
Ellen Toby Epstein
Joan Robin Falk
Ellen Josephine Finder
Peter Gary Fleischman
Nancy Ellen Forman
Jill Garson
David Barry Geffen
Marsha Robin Gelberg
Sheila Claire Gelman
Michael W. Gendler
Mina Gene Gerowin
Joel Jay Goldstein
Marjorie L. Graber
Steven Neal Hirsch
Susan H. Hochbaum
Donald Richard Hulnick

William Alan Kamer
Steven Barry Kase
Richard Brian Kaskawitz
Kenneth Alan Kleiger
Sim Andrew Kolliner
Meri R. Krassner
Carol B. Langsam
Robert Jay Lewinger
Robert Samuel Mittleman
Richard Lowell Perlman
Gerald Mark Reid
Larry Nolan Rein
Arlene Robin Sanford
Gil David Schwartz
Jeffrey Laurence Schwartz
John R. Scott
Nancy Ellen Socol
Daniel Paul Stillman
Sharon Ellen Strum
Sidney Ellen Wade
Judith Ann Wagner
Richard Hugh Waterman
Michael Alan Wintman

David Simon Yohalem

65. **The Van Etten Scholarship** established by the Women's Club of New Rochelle for a member of the senior class for further study. $150 awarded to **Aimara Cardenas.**

66. **The Pinebrook Homes Association Award** of a $50 bond to be awarded to a boy and a girl graduate who, in the opinion of the Awards Committee, have made the greatest overall contribution to the progress and development of our city through participation in civic affairs. Awarded to **Lisa Keller** and **Jay Lester Strongwater.**

67. **The Civil Service Association of the City School District of New Rochelle, N.Y. Scholarship.** This award is based on good citizenship and indication of promise in the field of endeavor and desire for further study. This award is established for a student in the vocational or business department. $200 is awarded to **Frank Walter Lore.**

68. **The Teachers Association of New Rochelle Scholarships,** awarded to members of the Class of 1969 who intend to enter the profession of teaching. $150 each awarded to **Roger William Sterner** and **Stephanie Elaine Weekes.**

69. **Scholarship** for one year to the **Art Students League of New York** in memory of Miss Mary Griggs, Art Supervisor in New Rochelle Schools for many years. Awarded to **Ellen Raquel Lebow.**

70. **The Natalie J. Gitlitz Memorial Award** to the person in the Business, Vocational, or General Program who distinguished himself as an outstanding student and who plans to further his education. This award is given in the name of Natalie J. Gitlitz in the hope that it will provide an added incentive and encouragement for that student to fulfill his educational and human potential. $100 awarded to **Philip Edward Buccolo.**

71. **The Leonard Talner Memorial Award** to the member of the class judged by the Class of 1969 to have done the most for and brought the most honor to the New Rochelle High School — awarded to **Eric Herman Vinson.**

72. **The Young Artists of New Rochelle Award** for 1969 to a talented and serious student choosing music as a profession. $250 awarded to **Abbe Ellen Harkavy.**

GRADUATES

GRADUATED IN AUGUST 1968

Michael Garret Abreu
Anthony Lamont Allen
Catherine Ann Anderson
Lloyd C. Beard
Arnold Willie Belton
Richard John Bookless
Joseph A. Brindisi
Timothy Michael Broder
Bert Arley Burtscher
Kent James Caparell
Anthony John Catalano
Philip D'Amore
Lewis Arthur Derry
Virginia Marie DeTorres
Michael Joseph DiLeo
Amerigo DiPietro
John DiRoma
Jamie Douglas
Ellen Toby Epstein

Gregory Lamont Gary
Jamie Joyce Greene
Joseph C. Gev..ts
Dennis Frank Gutt..rez
Allen Mark Hymans
John Howard Jackson
Brenda Mari. Johnson
Gary King
William J. Mahoney
Michelene E. Marrone
Thomas Cecil Mattison
John Steven Middleton
Robert Jerome Mollicone
Michael Peter Morceau
John J. Mazzullo
Richard James Pacifico
Anthony Nicholas Rafla
Pamela Lynn Reichert
Phyllis Ann Reichert

Margaret Anne Rice
Daniel John Romal
Barbara Ann Savasta
Vincent J. Scocchera, Jr.
Mark C. Shafer
Jane Shalvey
Robert Patrick Sheehy
Paul Frederic Shelton
Donald Joseph Sparacin
Arthur David Sterenberg
James Joseph Sundermeyer
Latanya Leanora Tyler
Frank Joseph Umbro
Mauro M. Viccaro
James Nicholas Vietro
Denise Washington
Donald William Weigand
Susan Ellen Witkin

CLASS OF 1969

President .... Eric Herman Vinson
Vice President .... Jonathan Edward Barnes
Secretary .... Steven Jay Koppel
Treasurer .... Jay Howard Goldstein

Mark Lewis Aaron
Nancy Louise Aborn
Deborah Tina Abramson
*Samuel Thomas Adenbaum
Doreen Ann Aiello
*Elizabeth Aisenberg
Elaine Michelle Albero
Robert Lee Alexander, Jr.
Michael John Alfano
Janis L. Allen
Michael David Almlof
Richard Kevin Alose
*Donald Bruce Alpert
Steven Gary Alpert
Owen David Altman
Elizabeth Alves
Andrew Vincent Amico
Dominick Amorosano
Denford Washington Anderson
Yvonne Marjorie Anderson
Alan Jay Antokal
Robert Norman Appelbaum

Jed Arkin
*Karen Ann Armiento
Arthur Norman Aronson
Marie Ann Arricale
*Alan Jeffrey Auerbach
Christina Margaretha Auman
Cheryl Ann Austin

Ilona Lois Bachelman
Robert Elliot Backer
Joanne Elizabeth Bailey
Loren Harriet Baily
Albert Balestrieri
Bruce Lee Barger
*Jonathan Edward Barnes
Ruth Natalie Barnes
Glenn Barnett
Jerrold Baron
Margaret Barone
*Joan Cynthia Barr
James Andrew Barrett
Douglas Alan Bartee

Robert Edgar Baruc
Richard Alan Bauling
Deborah Sari Beards
Dennis Michael Beavers
Karen Sue Bedney
Robert Samuel Begun
Alan Simeon Behrens
*Barton Tucker Belkin
*Denise Belkin
*Rita Belserene
John Stuart Benjamin
Robert Warren Benkwitt
Carole Ann Berard
Janice Deena Berchin
Sara Ann Berger
Stephen Jay Berger
*Terry G. Bergman
Mitchell I. Berke
Cathy Ann Berne
*Jacqueline Bernheimer
Jeffrey Louis Bernstein
*Jeremy Blair Bernstein

Sheryl Rona Bialo
Michael Bruce Bieber
George Felix Bing
John L. Bingman
Robert Michael Blanco
*Julie Blatt
Robert David Block
Keith Martin Bloomfield
Joshua T. Bloomgarden
*Joshua Paul Bogin
L. Amy Bonderow
Patricia Boone
Deborah Ann Booth
Aaron H. Bousel
Evadne Therese Boyd
Nathaniel Kannick Boyd, Jr.
*Michael Bradley
*Peter Israel Breger
Sharon Lynn Brickle
*Carol Ann Brod
Laura Gail Broder
Barry Richard Brown
Beverley Elaine Brown
Charles Calvin Brown
Patricia Claire Brown
*Barbara Ann Bruce
Solveig Bruun
Philip Edward Buccolo
Barbara Joyce Buchwalter
Ive John Budija
Ulrich Herbert Buntrock
Cynthia Lee Burgess
Joseph David Burke
*Deborah Adrienne Burroni
Ellen May Burstein
Mary Louise Bynum

Kenneth Thomas Cacase
Deborah Lee Cameron
*Leslie Jane Campagna
Jo-Ann Marie Campanella
Daniel Campbell
Virginia Sue Campbell
Anthony James Cancro, Jr.
Ernest Capalbo
Carol Rosemarie Caposela
Thomas Joseph Cappellino
John A. Carchietta
Aimara Cardenas
Michael Brian Carew
Patrick Anthony Carlino
Brigid Cathleen Carlson
Elizabeth Carol
Mario Carpanzano
Debra Marie Carr
Linda Jean Carrig
Guy Alonzo Carson
Kathy Jo Carson
Charles Thomas Carton
Frank Anthony Caruso
John Joseph Caruso
Vincent Albert Caruso
Gary Edward Caspi
Marc Steven Castle
Barbara Ann Catino
Patrick C. Catullo
James Cerasuolo
Anthony Cesario, Jr.
*Robin Chalek

Denise Angela Champion
Thomas Joseph Cheera
Richard Christopher Cherico
Dominic Chiera
Charles Dennis Chiodo
Valerie Holly Clark
Robert Claster
Diane Louise Claude
Robert Scharl Cocks
Jeff Cohen
Peter Arthur Cole
Gerald Allan Coleman
William Bruce Coleman
Roberta Coloday
Joseph Richard Colombo
Robert Thomas Connick
Susan Lynn Cooper
Daniel L. Correia
Victoria Jean Coughlin
Carole Mary Coviello
Linda Ann Cowart
Barbara Jean Cowen
Catherine Elizabeth Cox
Arthenia Edna Crawford
Robert John Creaturo
Louis Daniel Cristofaro
Harold G. Crocker
Wayne M. Curtis
Wanda Jane Cushnie

Genevieve Ann Marie D'Adamo
Jacqueline Dandey
Antonia Daniele
Frederic Armstrong Davidson, III
*Susan D. Davidson
*Jill Leslie Davis
Diane Divino De Bartolo
Kim Teresa De Beaumont
Glenn Decker
Michael Angelo De Clemente
Edmond Del Monte
Joseph Vincent De Luca
*Steven Demby
Michael Richard Demsey
Frances Pamela Denmark
Salvatore De Raffele
Brenda Marie De Renzis
Marianne Ellen De Rosa
Steve Desmet
Frances De Stefano
Frank A. Di Buono
Carol Jean Di Carmine
Thomas Di Marino
Joseph Di Paola
Marian Di Piazza
Angela J. Di Vito
Gay Doherty
Marjorie Dolores Dolson
Nicholas N. Donato, Jr.
Carol Ann D'Onofrio
Michael Louis D'Onofrio
Joseph Dorf, Jr
*Barbara Dorfman
Rosanne Doria
Walter Kevin Dougherty
Judith Irene Douglas
Dawn Alicia Dreyfuss
Patricia Anne Dyer
Laurel Anne Eccleston

Joan Marie Edler
Nancy Gail Edwards
Margaret Anne Eich
*Teresa Ann Eichler
Noel M. Elia
Lynne Patricia Ellison
*Judith H. Elman
Sandy Sue Elphand
Ruth Ellen Emmerich
Michael Kevin Emmerson
Helen Ann English
Abby Lynn Epstein
Veveline Erwin
Janet Louise Evans

Patricia Anne Fagan
John Hamilton Fairhall
*Joan Robin Falk
Ann Mary Fallshay
Kathie Leona Farrington
Elaine Karen Fein
*Patricia Lynn Feinman
Leslie Gail Feld
Robert Jay Feldman
*Shelley Lynne Feldman
Carolyn Jean Fentress
Barbara Ann Feola
Lorraine Ann Feola
Annette Ferstenberg
Richard Raymond Fetzer
William E. Fiedler
*Ellen Josephine Finder
Debra Helene Finette
Lawrence Neil Finkel
Jeanne Ellen Finkelstein
*Dena Finn
Robert Anthony Fiorito
Steven James Firkser
Jeffrey H. Fischer
Cheryl Lee Fissel
Barbara Ann Fiumara
Christopher Fiumara
*Michael David Fixler
Lewis Steven Fleischman
*Peter Gary Fleischman
Charles Eric Fletcher
Raymond Rodger Fookes
Dennis C. Foreman
Nancy Ellen Foreman
Jane E. Forster
Ernest John Fossa
Colette Yvonne Fowlkes
Phillip George Ivanhoe Francis
Michael Richard Frenz
*Lisa Sue Friedenberg
David Herman Fullman
Jeffrey Douglas Frankel
Mitchell D. Fried
*Laura Lynn Friedman
Frederick C. Froatz
John A. Frusciante
Lisa Margit Furer
Gerardo Puschetto

Anthony Daniel Galante
Cynthia Kathryn Gale
Gregory Walter Gale
Nancy Joyce Gamache
Nicola Gambardella

53. **The Louise Amonson Memorial Scholarships** of $50 each to two deserving athletes who are going on to college. Awarded to **Bruce Lee Barger** and **Nathaniel Kannick Boyd, Jr.**

54. **The Louis Lise Memorial Award,** presented by the New Rochelle Little League to a member of the Varsity Baseball Team who has shown outstanding dedication and improvement. Plaque awarded to **Accursio Ernest Generoso, Jr.**

55. **Michael Schwerner Award** to the two students who worked to eliminate the sickness of discrimination and the disease of prejudice. $5 each awarded to **Philip George Ivanhoe Francis** and **Loren Harriet Baily.** A plaque is to be installed in the lobby with the names of the winners inscribed on it annually.

56. **The Steven Mark Award** given in honor of one of the outstanding members of the Class of 1965 who has shown remarkable courage, determination and optimism in the face of adversity. A $25 bond is presented to **Brenda Joyce Rose.**

57. **The Richard Philip Kulick Memorial Awards** presented by Dr. and Mrs. Arthur Kulick in memory of their son, a graduate of New Rochelle High School, to a boy and girl in the senior class who have had to overcome problems during their high school years, to encourage the further growth and fulfillment of the students to whom they are awarded. Presented to **Cynthia Kathryn Gale** and **Richard Pocker.**

58. **The James G. Healey Memorial Award** given by Westchester Lodge #1079 of the International Association of Machinists and Aerospace Workers, AFL-CIO, in honor of James G. Healey, first president of the Lodge, to a student who has shown excellence in machine shop. A $25 bond is awarded to **Charles M. Italiano.**

59. **Tom Paine Lodge No. 2017, B'nai B'rith Award** to that member of the senior class who has made an outstanding effort during his attendance at New Rochelle High School to improve human relations among the student body. A $50 bond is awarded to **Eric Herman Vinson.**

60. **Pythian Friendship Awards** given by New Rochelle Lodge No. 592, Knights of Pythias, to a boy and a girl who are not enrolled in the college preparatory course — for excellence in citizenship, good character, and a friendly, considerate and helpful attitude in relations with students and faculty. A $25 bond is awarded to **Dennis C. Foreman** and **Janet Louise Evans.**

61. **The Joan Levine Memorial Award** of $25 given each year at Class Day by the friends of Joan Levine, Class of 1956, in her memory, to a girl in the senior class who has shown general excellence in academic achievement and extracurricular activities in her years at New Rochelle High School. Awarded to **Joan Falk.**

62. **The John F. Kennedy Memorial Citizenship Award** to the member of the class who, in the opinion of his teachers, has shown outstanding citizenship traits. A medallion struck in the likeness of our late President is awarded to **Peter Jay Sims.**

63. **American Legion Scholarship Awards** given by the New Rochelle Post No. 8. These are awarded on the basis of scholarship, with due consideration of other fine qualities such as honor, courage, leadership, and service. Medal and certificate awarded to **Sharon Ellen Strum** and **Jeremy Alan Wise.**

64. **The Albert Leonard Memorial Scholarship** in memory of Dr. Albert Leonard, former Superintendent of Schools, to assist a worthy student to meet the expenses of the freshman year in college. $100 awarded to **Michael Tadao Tsukada.**

42. The New Rochelle High School Parent Teacher Association Awards in Business Education for proficiency and skill:
    Accounting — $5 awarded to Robert James Smith
    Office Practice — $5 awarded to Stephanie Mary Pastore
    Secretarial Practice — $5 awarded to Graceann Simonetti
    Shorthand — $5 awarded to Joan Vicki Yankow

43. The Dr. Vern A. Frisch Award given by Mrs. Frisch in his honor to the student in the business department selected by the teachers of the department as the student of high scholarship, leadership and excellence of character. $25 awarded to Karen Louise Mann.

44. The New Rochelle High School Parent Teacher Association Awards in Vocational Education, Industrial Arts, and Fine Arts, for general proficiency and skill:
    Automotive Trades — $5 awarded to Robert Scharl Cocks
    Commercial Art — $5 awarded to Ellen Raquel Lebow
    Cosmetology — $5 awarded to Nancy Staropoli
    Electrical Trades — $5 awarded to James Carl Pugliese
    — $5 awarded to Joseph Vincent DeLuca
    Machine Trades — $5 awarded to Stephen Vincent Murphy
    Arts & Crafts — $5 awarded to Doris Helen Wood
    Fine Arts — $5 awarded to Dorothy Ann Herman
    Industrial Arts Electronics — $5 awarded to Charles Dennis Chiodo
    Industrial Arts Metal — $5 awarded to Nicholas N. Donato, Jr.
    Industrial Arts Wood — $5 awarded to Wayne D. Greene

45. The Cosmetology Teachers' Guild Medal for outstanding service and achievement, awarded to Brenda Marie DeRenzis.

46. The New Rochelle High School Cosmetology Medal for general excellence in this field awarded to Karole Margaret Liptak.

47. The Cosmetology Gold Pin Award for outstanding achievement in this field awarded to Lillian Elizabeth Gerardi.

48. The Fashion Trades Teachers' Guild Key for fashion designing, awarded to Ann Mary Fallshay.

49. The New Rochelle High School Awards for excellence in Textiles: Gold medal awarded to Michelle Linda Martens, gold pin to Nadine Lois Ochacher.

50. The Standard Star Press Club Merit Award based on quality of work and granted to an outstanding member of the Press Club. Medal awarded to Michelle Harvey Moss.

51. The Herman Falk, Jr. Memorial Medal presented to the senior who has been outstanding in track, in memory of a graduate of New Rochelle High School who was a member of the track team. He died in Korea after two years in a prison camp. Awarded to Steven Gary Alpert.

52. The Thelbert James Award, given by Spoken Arts, Inc., to a student who has shown exceptionally good sportsmanship and spirit as an athlete, in memory of Thelbert James who gave his life for his country in Vietnam before he had a chance to enjoy the fruits of his life. Gary Stephen Monteferante is awarded $40.

30. The Honorary Science Award presented by Bausch and Lomb Optical Company to that member of the senior class who has made outstanding achievement in three branches of science: biology, chemistry and physics; and who seems best fitted psychologically to pursue a scientific career. Medal awarded to Alan Jeffrey Auerbach.

31. The Grubel Memorial Prize, given in memory of Philip Grabel of Grabel's Pharmacy, to the student with the highest achievement in science over a period of three years. $25 awarded to Peter Gary Fleischman.

32. The P.T.A. of New Rochelle High School Award to the senior who has done the most outstanding work in biology. $10 awarded to Steven Goldfinger.

33. The P.T.A. of New Rochelle High School Award to the senior who has done the most outstanding work in chemistry. $10 awarded to Julie Blatt.

34. The P.T.A. of New Rochelle High School Award to the senior who has done the most outstanding work in physics. $10 awarded to Donald Bruce Alpert.

35. The Rensselaer Polytechnic Institute Alumni Association Medal for the highest rating in mathematics and science awarded in the junior year to Donald Bruce Alpert.

36. The P.T.A. of New Rochelle High School Award conferred upon a senior for general excellence in the honors sequence of mathematics courses. $10 awarded to Peter Gary Fleischman.

37. The P.T.A. of New Rochelle High School Award conferred upon the senior who has completed four or five years in the regular mathematics program and demonstrated unusual insight, skill, and interest. $10 awarded to Nancy Ellen Socol.

38. The Edward A. Sper Memorial Award given by Mrs. Sper in honor of her husband, to the senior who has shown most growth in mathematics through interest and application. $15 awarded to Alan Jeffrey Auerbach.

39. The Mathematical Association of America Award to the senior with the highest score in New Rochelle High School in the Annual High School Mathematics Contest. Pin awarded to Peter Gary Fleischman.

40. The Mrs. Louis Bernstein Business Service Award given by the League of Women Voters for outstanding service to school and community. $10 is awarded to Janet Louise Evans.

41. Distributive Education Awards:
    R. H. Macy Company — to the outstanding student in Distributive Education — $25 to Dennis C. Foreman

    Sears Roebuck Company — for outstanding work in Display — $25 to Diane DeBartolo

    F. W. Woolworth Company — for outstanding work in Advertising — $10 to Christopher Fiumara

    National Bank of Westchester — for outstanding work in Personnel — $10 to Marie Ann Arricale

    Leonard Talner Jewelers — for outstanding work in Sales — $10 to Charles Brown

    Mendelsohn's Luggage Company — for outstanding work in Store Control — $10 to Philip Edward Buccolo

14. **The General Louis Blenker Unit 125, Steuben Society of America** presents to the best student in American history a prize of a silver medal and $15 to **Gil David Schwartz.** Honorable Mention to **Joan Falk** and **Richard Lowell Perlman.**

15. **The K. B. Weissman Prizes in American History** emphasizing research and critical analysis. First prizes of $25 each awarded to **David Alan Levine** and **Jeffrey Laurence Schwartz;** second prizes of $15 each awarded to **Joshua Paul Bogin** and **Nancy Ellen Socol;** third prizes of $10 each awarded to **Frederick Sanford Harris** and **Eliot Joel Locitzer;** Honorable Mention to **Dena Finn** and **George Mitchell Kahn.**

16. **The Robert Alan Shwitzer Memorial Prize** given by the family of Robert Alan Shwitzer, Class of 1941. Awarded for keen interest in and study of the broader and deeper significance of events in American history. Awarded to **William Alan Kamer;** Honorable Mention to **Richard Kaskawits** and **Sim Andrew Kolliner.**

17. **The Sylva A. Kunce Memorial Award** of $10 to a student from the psychology classes who demonstrates the most improvement and growth in understanding himself and others. Awarded to **Miranda Lee.**

18. **The Social Studies Department Awards in Psychology** for excellence and interest in the subject. $5 each awarded to **Emily Beth Rosenblum** and **Doris Helen Wood.**

19. **The P.T.A. of New Rochelle High School Award** for the best record in Problems of American Democracy. $5 each awarded to **Loren Harriet Baily** and **Stephen Jay Berger.** Honorable Mention to **Ellen Marcia Glasser, Jane Debra Levy** and **Jeffrey Ephraim Strum.**

20. **The Frederick Julian Steinhardt French Prize of $15** given to the senior having the highest average in third year French by Mr. Samuel C. Steinhardt in honor of his son. Awarded to **Dulce Herrera.**

21. **The P.T.A. of New Rochelle High School Award** to the senior having the highest average in fourth year Spanish. $10 awarded to **Carol Ann Brod.**

22. **The P.T.A. of New Rochelle High School Award** to the senior having the highest average in third year Spanish. $10 awarded to **Marjorie Joan Miller.**

23. **The P.T.A. of New Rochelle High School Award** to the senior having the highest average in second year Spanish. $10 awarded to **Linda Miriam Yowell.**

24. **The P.T.A. of New Rochelle High School Award** to the senior having the highest average in second year Latin. $10 awarded to **Dena Finn.**

25. **The P.T.A. of New Rochelle High School Award** for excellence in fourth year Latin. $10 awarded to **Saran Saul Rosner.**

26. **The Marcia Weinstein Prize** given by the Marcia Weinstein Chapter of Lupus Erythmatosus Foundation, Inc., in memory of Marcia Weinstein of the Class of 1958, for excellence in fourth year French. $15 awarded to **Robert Jack Wolf.**

27. **The P.T.A. of New Rochelle High School Award** to the senior who has done the most outstanding work in French 5. $10 awarded to **Julie Blatt.**

28. **Russian Prizes** for general excellence in second year Russian. Books donated by Four Continents Book Shop awarded to **Julie Blatt** and **Peter Gary Fleischman.**

29. **American Association of Teachers of French Awards:** In the Westchester County competition in fifth level, second prize was won by **Barbara Ann Bruce.**

Susan Mary Roberts
Helen Butler Robin
George Andrew Robinson
Priscilla Robinson
Wayne Alan Robinson
Jan Rocco
Douglas Paul Rock
Elaine Constance Rocos
Michael Rodbell
James Roddy
Paula Jean Roddy
Gabriel Romaine, Jr.
Stephen Joseph Romano
*Patricia Lynn Roper
Jo Ann Constance Rorus
Andrew Frederick Rose
Brenda Joyce Rose
Richard Bruce Rose
Michael B. Rosen
Michael William Rosen
*Emily Beth Rosenblum
David Eric Rosengren
*Saran Saul Rosner
*Joan Carol Ross
Michael Felix Rossi
Ronald Fred Rossman
*Jane Ellen Roth
Joan Ellen Rothberg
Patricia Dianne Royster
Inese G. Rudzitis
Felix Ruiz, Jr.
Richard Rumph, Jr.

*Linda Karen Sacainy
Esther M. Sacco
Lynda Marie Saccone
Stephen Salvatore
John Samalot
Susan Elizabeth Samela
Irving Lee Samuels
*Arlene Robin Sanford
*Peter Steven Saretsky
Francis Geraldine Savino
Karen Helene Sawyer
Dennis Michael Sayer
Robert William Schaefer
Theresa Diane Schappert
Marinus Cornelius Schippers
*Alan B. Schiftman
Christine Schmitz
Steven Alan Schnitzer
Ronald Arthur Schoenberr
Joan Ilene Schustack
*Hildi Barbara Schwade
Barbara Schwartz
*Gil David Schwartz
*Jeffrey Laurence Schwartz
Karen Barbara Schwartz
*John R. Scott
Laurie Ann Seiden
*June Clare Semenza
*Jennifer Leigh Seney
*Gary Donald Shapiro
Lori Hope Shapiro
*Diane Ellen Shaw
Michael Joseph Shea
Elizabeth Lambert Sheils
Karen L. Sheiner
Margaret Ann Sheridan

*Patricia Lynn Sherman
Karen Maria Sith
Melvyn Barry Siegel
Jo Anne Josephine Signorelli
John Patrick Signorelli
Margarete Mary Silvan
Diane Ruth Silverman
Gail Ellen Silverman
*Neal Gordon Simon
*Graceann Simonetti
*Peter Jay Sims
*Elise Lynn Siniak
*Margaret Ann Sipser
Paul Allen Sklar
Lisa Cathy Smith
Robert James Smith
Stephen Drew Smith
Susan Lynne Smith
*Nancy Ellen Socol
Jeffrey Howard Solomon
Ellen Spallazzi
Deniese Lee Spalter
*Adrienne Marcia Specher
Jeffrey Spetler
Renee E. Spiegel
*Donald Alan Spitzer
Victoria Anne Sposeto
*Nordeen M. Squilla
John Austin Stainkamp
Deborah Jane Stang
Robert Ralph Stanziale
Gloria Staropoli
Nancy Staropoli
*Patricia Jane Steckler
Elliot Ricky Steinberg
Michele Donna Steinberg
*Joseph Jay Stern
*June Michelle Stern
*Nancy Lynn Stern
Roger William Sterner
*Daniel Paul Stillman
Vicki Ellen Stillman
*Steven Marc Stoller
Sandy Stollerman
Barbara Ann Strazza
*Jay Lester Strongwater
Joseph A. Strother, Jr.
Ronald Leonard Strother
Jeffrey Ephraim Strum
*Sharon Ellen Strum
Donna A. Sturman
Jessica Margaret Stutz
Janice Sugarman
Thomas L. Sullivan
Gary Salvatore Summo
Allan Roy Sussberg
Brian Howard Sussman
Jay Ronald Sussman
Steven Mark Sussman
Fern Suval

Barbara Lynn Taibi
Leslie Joy Tamis
Mitchell Charles Tander
Ronald Karl Taphorn
Diane Christine Tarricone
Guy Weldon Tatum, Jr.
Armentha Noel Taylor
Denise Karin Taylor

Dorothy Mary Telesco
Anthony Terracciano
Barbara Elizabeth Thomas
Gregory Floyd Thomas
Joseph Thomas, Jr.
William George Tierney
Debra Faye Tobias
Ronald Blake Tobin
Gloria Ines Tobon
Vito Torchia
Rosanne Torricelli
Marsha Valerie Townes
Anthony Vincent Towsley
*Tiana Trattner
Michael Tadao Tsukada
Helen Elizabeth Tulloch
Jill Leslie Turner
Leslie Carolyn Twyeffort

*Marilyn Sue Ullman
Amy Beth Umansky
Victoria B. Unschuld
Susan Linda Utsch

Denise Patricia Vaccaro
Walter Henry Vail
Robert Valenti
Mauro Anthony Viccaro
Carmen Nicholas Vigliotti
John Joseph Vilasi
Eric Herman Vinson

Mary Elaine Wade
*Sidney Ellen Wade
*Judith Ann Wagner
Bruce Peter Wainer
Hazel Darnel Walker
Gail Henrietta Waller
Randall William Wallin
Carolyn Wander
*Richard Hugh Waterman
Barbara A. Watkins
Frances Ligia Weaver
Dodbrook Evelyn Weekes
Stephanie Elaine Weekes
Robert Weinberger
Susan Robin Weiner
Gilbert Nehemi Weiser
Jessica Naomi Weiss
Alan Frederick Weissman
Mindy April Weissman
Bonnie L. Welsh
Bruce Alvin Wessel
Roberta Hellene Whalen
Patricia Ann Wheeler
Patrick Joseph Wheeler
Roger Phillip Wheeler
Aretha Whitley
Sara Debra Wilkenfeld
Ormond Anthony Wille, III
Alfred Clifton Williams
Brenda Juanita Williams
Delilah T. Williams
Gladstone L. Williams
Joseph Albert Williams, Jr.
Michelle Williams
Wendy Carol Willinger
*Michael Alan Wintman
*Jeremy Alan Wise

*Linda Susan Wohl
Lawrence Jeffrey Wolf
*Robert Jack Wolf
*Kathy S. Wolff
John Louis Wolfsie
*Linda Joan Wolfsie
Peter Allan Wolfsie
John Frederick Wolgast
*Carole Edith Wollman
Peter David Wolstein
Doris Helen Wood
Frances Wood

Joseph R. Woodward, Jr.

*Joan Vicki Yankow
Peter F. Yellin
Edward Masis Yeterian
*David Simon Yohalem
Kenneth Jeffrey Young
Robert Bruce Younger
*Linda Miriam Yowell
Deborah Yuen
Richard Warren Yustman
Daniel Zaffino

Edward Zaffino
*Neil Henry Zane
Daniel James Zarrilli
Alfonso Ziccardi
Elena Gae Zimmerman
Steven Barry Ziplow
Richard Joseph Zippilli
Joan Ellen Zirolnik
*Barry Zuckerman
Lorna Helen Zuzulo

*Indicates membership in National Honor Society

OCCUPATIONAL EDUCATION CERTIFICATE

Stephen Dennis Smith

NEW ROCHELLE HIGH SCHOOL
NEW YORK STATE REGENTS SCHOLARSHIP WINNERS

Donald B. Alpert
Alan J. Auerbach
Glenn Barnett
Rita Belserene
Terry G. Bergman
Julie Blatt
Joshua P. Bogin
Peter I. Breger
Barbara F. Dorfman
Teresa A. Eichler
Abby L. Epstein
John H. Fairhall
Ellen J. Finder
Peter G. Fleischman
David B. Geffen
Michael W. Gendler
Mina G. Gerowin
Steven H. Goldfinger
Kenneth S. Goldrich
Jay H. Goldstein
Joel J. Goldstein

Arnold S. Gordon
Marjorie L. Graber
Ralph J. Guggenheim
Frederick Harris
Steven N. Hirsch
Donald H. Hulnick
Nancy Jacobs
William A. Kamer
Steven B. Kase
Richard B. Kaskawits
Robert J. Katz
Kenneth A. Klinger
Andrew Kolliner
Carol B. Langsam
Miranda Lee
Robert J. Lewinger
Eliot J. Locitzer
Robert S. Mittleman
Richard Orentzel
John M. O'Toole
Barry S. Paul

Richard L. Perlman
Henry J. Posner
Robert E. Pressberg
Alan J. Pue
Gerald M. Reid
Larry N. Rein
Saran S. Rosner
Arlene R. Sanford
Peter S. Saretsky
Gil D. Schwartz
Jeffrey L. Schwartz
Peter J. Sims
Nancy E. Socol
Joseph J. Stern
Daniel P. Stillman
Judith A. Wagner
Richard H. Waterman
Linda S. Wohl
Lawrence J. Wolf
David S. Yohalem
Linda Yowell

SENIOR AWARDS — Class of 1969

1. **Graduation Awards** presented for outstanding and long participation in the instrumental groups of the school. $5 is awarded to each of the following: **Michael Bruce Bieber, Frank Anthony Caruso, Steven Demby, Marian DiPiazza, Teresa Ann Eichler, Robert Lawrence Johnson, George Mitchell Kahn, Eliot Joel Locitzer, Yvonne Roberta McClelland.**

2. **The Tillie and Max Goldstein Memorial Award** to the outstanding member of the band and orchestra over a period of years. $10 awarded to **Charles Morgan LeCount, Jr.**

3. **The Harold N. Finkelstein Memorial Award** for outstanding contributions to the New Rochelle High School instrumental music program. $25 awarded to **Daniel Campbell.**

4. **The Choral Department Graduation Awards** to seniors who have contributed efficiently and loyally to the success of New Rochelle High School choirs and varied musical activities. $5 each awarded to **Karen Sue Bedney, Joshua Paul Bogin, Daniel Campbell, Teresa Ann Eichler, Ralph J. Guggenheim, George Mitchell Kahn, Andrew Paul Kraus, Anna Elizabeth Novikoff, Joan Carol Ross, Leslie Carolyn Twyeffort.**

5. **The Musical Scholarship Award** of $50 presented by the officers and members of the Music Teachers Council of New Rochelle. This award is given to an academic student who intends to continue his or her music education and who has participated very successfully in the vocal and instrumental music activities of the school. Awarded to **Abbe Ellen Harkavy.**

6. **The Philharmonic Society of Westchester Award** to the most outstanding music student in the senior class. A plaque is presented to **Abbe Ellen Harkavy.**

7. **The Young Artists of New Rochelle Executive Board** gives a special award to the student who for several years has contributed greatly to the success of our concerts by her cooperation, personality and musicianship. $50 awarded to **Teresa Ann Eichler.**

8. **The Lincoln Center Student Award Winners** of the Class of 1969 from New Rochelle High School are **Teresa Ann Eichler, Abbe Ellen Harkavy, Alan James Pue, Patricia Lynn Sherman.**

9. **The Frederick Julian Steinhardt English Prize** of $15 given by Mr. Samuel C. Steinhardt in honor of his son, Class of 1926, for the best work in a contest in original English composition. Awarded to **Joel J. Goldstein.**

10. **The P.T.A. of New Rochelle High School Award** for general excellence in English. $5 each awarded to **Julie Blatt** and **Joan Robin Falk.**

11. **The Journalism Award** of $10 to the student who, through his effort, has done most to further the journalistic achievements of New Rochelle High School. $5 each awarded to **Joan Robin Falk** and **Lisa Keller.**

12. **The Spoken Arts, Inc. Prize in Literature** awarded to the boy and girl who, in the judgment of the English department, show outstanding promise in the study of English. $25 bond awarded to **Constance Kramer** and **Gil David Schwartz.**

13. **The Davis Memoral Prize** given in memory of George T. Davis, one of New Rochelle's most honored citizens. Awarded for excellence in American history to **Saran Saul Rosner.** Honorable Mention to **Gary Donald Shapiro** and **Mina Gene Gerowin.**

As we returned for our senior year. Most of the classes were now being held in the portable trailers behind the school. Most of the students were now assigned to either attending school in the morning or attending class in the afternoon. Double session was being used due to the lack of space as re-construction had begun as well.

Music was also a big part of my High School Years. I learned the guitar and bought my 1969 Fender Telecaster from Caruso's Music Store and soon myself with Johnny Cacciatore singing lead along with Sal DeRaffele on Bass Guitar, Freddy Paganico on Guitar and Bill Lauer on drums (then replaced by Jack DeRosa when Bill left) I named the Band "The Lott" after my beautiful English Teacher Miss Delott....We had some good times, playing dances, battle of the bands and parties.

Another major event going on wasn't in the "West" or at New Rochelle High School. It was the Vietnam War. No need to talk about the complexity of the war and it's protocol of the military. But the big thing was what they called "The Draft Lottery" for the selective service draft into the military.

Graduation in June of 1969 ended with thoughts of was I joining the Military Reserves or entering to see what my number would be in the Draft Lottery. I explored the idea of joining the reserves while my father drove me to Whitehall Street to take all the tests for military qualification acceptance. I received my letter of admission 6 months later but I chose to wait for my draft number and declined the offer of joining the military. My draft number was (352).

My childhood good friends Danny Costa & Mauro Viccaro chose to join the United States Marines.

Chapter (15)

Outside the "West"

By now in writing this book you have the feel how special "The West" neighborhood is compared to the rest of the City of New Rochelle neighborhood's. I'm not saying as the saying goes "The West is the Best"— I'm just saying "The West' was a city in it's self. But it also because of it's geography of homes it had a very close nit of everyone looking out for each other and everyone was like family. Again, not to disclose a negative displeasure towards the South, East, Central and North end of New Rochelle because they too have character, charm, diversity, friendly neighbors and beautiful homes and landscape in their neighborhoods.

The South End of New Rochelle with it's beautiful neighborhoods and parks that reach and extend to the waters of the Long Island Sound. The South End has the Beach Clubs, Glen Island Beach with it's history of Castle's and the Glen Island Casino that was the home of the Big Band Era with Ozzie Nelson, Charlie Barnet, Les Brown, Dorsey Brothers. There is also a rumor that Frank Sinatra stopped by and sang one night. There is the famous 1939 radio broadcast's of Glenn Miller from the main dining room. The South has Eddie Foy Park from the Movie "The 7 Little Foys"—It has Leno's Clam bar known as "Greasy Nick's—family related to comedian/actor and TV personality Jay Leno. Jay himself lived in the South End of New Rochelle as he attended Trinity Elementary School in 3rd & 4th grade before moving to the New England area. The South End was once the home to NY Yankees Lou Gehrig while he was winning all those world championships.

As beautiful as the South End is—it doesn't have the "West End" City among a City feeling.

It is what it is a Beautiful Neighborhood.

The East End of New Rochelle. A neighborhood of small but quant homes lined with beautiful flowers, green grass and brush. Back in the 50's and 60's it had a small stretch of stores along East Main St. It's proximity to Main St made it walk able to the shopping but not much in the line of having it's own character of a neighborhood of shops. It had the old Stephenson Elementary School (that was eventually knocked down and taken away) with it's small playground for the kids enjoyment. The playground had it's share of basketball courts and activities and in the hot summers the sprinklers kept the kids cool. A wonderful area the East End is. As I mentioned lovely homes and nice quite area and I'm sure friendly neighbors. A very nice place to live and bring up a family. But it lacks the closeness and charm "The West" always endured. Again not a knock on the East End. As mentioned with the South End.

The East End is what it is a Beautiful Neighborhood.

The Central part of New Rochelle along the North Ave corridor that extended in the Rochelle Park/Heights and The Boulevard section behind Iona College. What a gorgeous row of homes, mansions along the hills with Rochelle Park right in the middle of it all. Eventually the home to the stars of stage and screen Ossie Davis and Ruby Dee along with many other artists, composers and actors.

The North End of New Rochelle has it's lavish homes now but back in the 50's and 60's there were a lot of farms up there off Quaker Ridge Rd, Daisy Farms and back into the Ward Acres area. I was even told off Quaker Ridge there was a horse track to exercise and run to train horses. There was Cherry lawn that had it's golf range. Except for Ward acres that was donated to the City (I Believe) all those farms and open land are now all as I said lavish one family mostly ranch homes.

People like baseball great Willie Mays lived in the North End. Opera Singer Robert Merrill, Another baseball great Frankie Frisch, Marty Glickman Sports Announcer/Olympic runner, William Randolph Hearst Newspaper Baron, Carl Reiner actor/producer, Norman Rockwell lived on

Lord Kitchener Rd....and the made for TV Sitcom Show—Rob and Laura Petrie—"The Dick Van Dyke Show" with Mary Tyler Moore.

Main Street, New Rochelle. Good ole days of the 50's-60's—I don't remember the trolley cars but I do remember the remains of the tracks in the middle of the streets as they used to pop up from time to time from underneath the asphalt on the street.

The good ole days when Main St. and Huguenot St. that ran parallel to each other with the cross streets like Division, Mechanic, Lawton etc all flourished with stores and business's and saloons. Police on corners directing traffic. Three Movie theaters, clothing stores, shoe stores, Department Stores, Robert Hall

CHAPTER (16)

The Way it was Through the Eyes of "Illustrations"

As we look at illustrations through newspaper clippings or old post cards sometimes we all see something different. As we look and reminisce at the pictures we see how it was so many many years ago. It brings us back to those memories of the way it was through your eyes! Time has changed, the neighborhood has changed, people have changed but the memories last for a life time!

As the saying goes:

St. Gabes

Old Library

P.O.

College of St. Angela, New Rochelle, N.Y.

Hudson Park

Old City Hall

Hospital

**The
"WEST"
is the
Best**

CHAPTER (17)

Can't Ignore the (4) Core
Gentleman from the "West"

Nick Trotta—Paul Sarachelli—William DeLuca—Peter Parente

4-Core

Although these (4) gentleman do not live in the "West" any longer and although they are younger then myself I cannot ignore their community roots of the "West End" of New Rochelle. They came after me and their growing and adolescent days extend into the 70's and probably the 80's as opposed to my 50's-60's. But there up-bringing does not change as they experienced the same neighborhood as I have and with fond memories of family and friends rejoice the fact that they grew up in the "West End" of New Rochelle.

I write about these men and believe me I can sit here for years and write about a lot of good men & woman past (as I did in previous chapters) and present that did and do so much in life and for the community of

"West" New Rochelle. As the title says I *cannot ignore* these (4) Gentleman of the "West" and their patron good deeds for the community at large: The residents, Civic Organizations, Boy's & Girl's Club, Saint Joseph Church etc.

Trotta

Mr. Nick Trotta, grew up in the "West"—went to school in the "West" and graduated from Iona College. His dream was to be a United States Secret Service Agent. That dream came through and before you know it Nick found himself in Washington, DC at the White House at the side of the President of the United States.

You see there are a lot of important jobs that are full of responsibility including police, fire, emergency workers, doctors, nurses etc. Jobs where you risk your life. But as a Secret Service Agent you not only risk your life but you put your life on the line by giving up your life as you are required to take a "bullet" as you guard the Commander and Chief—The President of the United States. That my friend is something very special, and you have to be special as the President must feel comfortable and very trust worthy with his personal agents. Nick gained the trust and respect from all (4) President's he worked for as he should be very proud as he made all of his family, friends proud to see the kid from the "West End" shown on the screen with the President from all four corners of the world!

Nick served for 30 years with the Secret Service retiring as Assistant Director. Nick served with dignity, honor, pride and strong faith from Father Joseph DiSanto. Everywhere he went with the President of the United States he wore his "West End" family & friends on his sleeve never forgetting his roots of the "West"!

Mr. Paul Sarachelli, from the "West End" of New Rochelle. A member of the 3rd Street Boys. People know him as a true dedicated friend and good family man. I always known him as the kind of guy that lived by the motto "Do the Right Thing"—"Show Respect—Gain Respect" A hard working family man that always for many years found time to commit to the "West End" by helping to raise money for the Boy's and Girls' Club and Saint Joseph Church. Countless hours of preparing and coordinating all kind of events raising thousands of dollars for some 20 years!

Paulie

Paulie (as most of us know him by) is not shy to honor a neighbor or a friend from the "West" to show how proud us "West Enders" are of someone that gained recognition or found some sort of fame from their job or there duty as a community activist.

Paul Sarachelli will always be known and I'm sure he will continue to support the "West"—the neighbors, friends, family the church and all civic organizations. Paulie is a man of his word who would go through a wall to help and assist someone to the best of his ability.

You need Paulie—No hesitation—He is there for you!

"Always their for you".... *"Show Respect—Gain Respect"*

Billy

William "Billy" DeLuca. When they told me Billy never forgot where he came from even though he is highly successful in the private sector as an Executive Manager for a million dollar company. Well, as I found out as many others have that to be so true it is very difficult to explain how true it is. But when you speak to Billy you find that warm personality making one comfortable in his presence.

Everyone loves Billy from a young kid running around the Boy's Club and around the "West" to rising as Senior Vice President of Sales and Marketing for Manhattan Beer Distributors. He has made his family, friends and everyone proud of his accomplishments and I got to say everyone is so very happy for him.

Billy still with his boyish looks is a tremendous family man and a lovable neighbor in his Town.

Anyone that knows Billy knows the many things he has done for everyone. Any sort of event going on Billy was gracious in helping as he found time to assist, speak and be there no matter how busy his schedule is. He too was there for the Church, the Boy's Club, Veterans, many civic organizations and everyone's personal events.

We could only applaud Billy and say "Thank You" as you never forgot your roots and where you came from! We could never re-pay Billy but only to admire his unselfish acts of being a great guy to us all.

On a personal note: "Thank You" Billy....

Congratulations to Billy's family as they raised a "Saint" who is proud to say he is from "West" New Rochelle.

Parente

Peter Parente—An amazing "Great American"—A true patriotic American through and through. A veteran of the United States Marines having served in Desert Storm. The American Flag fly's among his tall strut of dignity of love of Country, Family, Friends and the "West End" of New Rochelle. Grown into a long time family business Peter takes a strong pride of taking care of each individual customer as it was his own family as well as his friends when in need. Peter has been their for the Boy's & Girl's Club—A strong supporter of St. Joseph Church each year helping to raise money at the annual Feast.

A main stay of support for the Veterans of New Rochelle who believes in "Don't Tread On Me" motto as he has demonstrated to everyone! He brought the great "Memorial Day" Parade to New Rochelle. With all his hard work and all his support from his Family, New Rochelle staff and Elected Officials and devoted Friends makes it one of the best in the tri-state area.

A true leader who believes so deeply to his roots of "West" New Rochelle as he reaches out to saving the "Armory" on East Main St. from the ruins that has as much of a part of the history as the Huguenots that settled in New Rochelle some 300 years ago. The respect and dignity are planted in your heart and we Thank You Mr. Parente for your service to this Country and your dedicated volunteer service to the "West End" and to the New Rochelle residents as well as your patriotism to the United States of America.

"God Bless" you, our Veterans, our Troops and the USA!

CHAPTER (18)

Where am I Today?

Where am I today?—well after 34 years in Law Enforcement and now retired and having spent 29 years of my life with the Department of Correction I say Thank You as I found a good life among family and friends and acquaintances.

I found a nitch as a Radio Broadcaster as I continue with Talk & Music Radio since 1998.

I say Thank You to my side kick, friend and partner on the radio Ms. Tonny "G"....Thank You and foremost to Whitney Media CEO/President my mentor Mr. William O'Shaughnessy. Thank you to the wonderful staff Cindy Gallagher, Don Stevens, David & Mathew O'Shaughnessy, Kevin Elliot, John Harper, Judy Freemont, Richard Littlejohn, Jerryl Bell, Maggie Hernandez, and many others that I worked with at WVOX for so many years especially all different engineer/board operators—Debbie, Nick, Chris, Jovan, Big John and Steven Tito...Thank You to Bob Schafer and the late Joe Candria for my start as a guest on their radio show.... Thank You to former WVOX Program Director Matt Deutsch....Thank You to all the listeners, callers that made the show....Thank you to Eileen Mason, Linda Bafaro, Sharon "The Bunnie" and even Bernie for taking time out to come answer the telephone for Sunday song dedication/request for the oldies music radio show....Thank You to all the radio sponsors, especially the one and only Mr. William DeLuca from Manhattan Beer

Distributors and of course Frank Lore and Paul Sarachelli. I have to say how blessed I am to M-Cee oldies concert shows to bring out on stage the singing performers that I admired from the music of the 50's & 60's....Thank You to Nick Ciarmela, John Wheelen, Joe Cavanna for the opportunity to meet & greet the stars....

Thank You to all my supporters that were there for me for my birthday's and dance parties (you know who you are) all through the years especially Vic Sabatini and Michael Bello.

So as I finish this chapter and this book I leave you with these words of encouragement—wisdom and thought...

The same departing words when signing off on the radio:

God Bless You
God Bless The United States
God Bless Our Troops
—Hug Someone Today—
Keep That Smile On Your Face
<<<IMAGE>>>—And Remember—<<<IMAGE>>>
Every Meal Is A Blessing
Every Day Say "Thank You"
And—Don't Ever Forget—
"I Love You More Today Then Yesterday"

God Bless You
God Bless The United States
God Bless Our Troops
- Hug Someone Today -
Keep That Smile On Your Face
- And Remember -
Every Meal Is A Blessing
Every Day Say "Thank You"
And - Don't Ever Forget -
"I Love You More Today Then Yesterday"

Me

In Conclusion

In conclusion, please bare with me my spelling and my writing. I also ask please, remember this writing is in form of "My Memoirs." My thoughts and my memory of people, places and things. I wanted to write this book from memory, yes I could of put in many years of research by speaking with the old timers, friends and anyone that came out of the "West End" of New Rochelle. But I wanted to do it my way by sitting down and reflecting, reminiscing and searching from my heart and soul of what I remember about the "West."

So I ask you to be patient, If I forgot a name or if I spelt a name wrong, if I mistakenly got the wrong name mixed up with a person or business again please don't hold me to the wall of ignorance and say that is not the way it was. Correct me if you wish but again I wanted to write this book as my memoirs and wonderful thoughts of the people, places and things of growing up in "West End" of New Rochelle, New York in the 50's and 60's

I hope you enjoy my ride down memory lane with the writing of this Book!—I Thank You for Reading it and again I hope it brought back the many joyous childhood and youth days memories of growing up in the "West" as it did for me—God Bless the "West End"

Dennis M. Nardone

Italian Family

Printed in the USA
CPSIA information can be obtained
at www.ICGtesting.com
LVHW081930130224
771795LV00005B/80